THE MARROW OF TRUE JUSTIFICATION

.

THE
MARROW
OF
TRUE JUSTIFICATION:
OR,
JUSTIFICATION without WORKS.

Containing the substance of Two Sermons lately preached
on *Rom.* 4.5. And by the Importunity of some gracious
Christians, now published with some Additions.

WHEREIN

The Nature of Justification, is opened,
as it hath been formerly asserted
by all sound Protestants; and the present prevailing
Errors against the said Doctrine, detected.

By BENJAMIN KEACH, Pastor of a
Church of Christ, Meeting at *Horsly-Down, Southwark.*

---

*I will raise unto David a righteous Branch: and this is the name
whereby he shall be called, Jehovah, our Righteousness, Jer. 23.5,6.*

Justificatio est Doctrina stantis & cadentis Ecclesiae, *saith* Luther.

Solid Ground Christian Books
Birmingham, Alabama USA
April 2007

Solid Ground Christian Books
715 Oak Grove Road
Birmingham, AL 35209
205-443-0311
sgcb@charter.net
http://solid-ground-books.com

THE MARROW OF TRUE JUSTIFICATION

Benjamin Keach (1640-1704)

First published in 1692

First Solid Ground edition April 2007

Special Thanks to Jim Carnes of Memphis, TN for his
vision and faithful labors to see this project completed.

Cover design by Borgo Design, Tuscaloosa, AL.
Contact them at borgogirl@bellsouth.net

ISBN: 1-59925-114-0

TABLE OF CONTENTS

THE EPISTLE DEDICATORY

To all who desire to be found in the Righteousness of Christ, and count their own but as Dung in comparison thereof; particularly to the Congregation, Meeting at *Horsly-Down*, the Hearers of these Sermons, Grace, Mercy, and Peace be multiplied.

Brethren,

As I was put upon preaching on this great Subject; so I am satisfied it was at a very seasonable Hour, that Doctrine being greatly struck at by too many Persons, though of different Sentiment: in many Points of Religion. And as it was well accepted by you, who heard these Sermons (and the others that followed) when preach'd; and having been prevail'd with to publish these in the World, so I hope some may receive Advantage hereby: Though for the meanness of the Author, and weakness of the Work, they may not meet with that Entertainment from some as the Subject deserves; yet for your sakes whose Souls are committed to my Charge, and for whom I must give Account to the great Shepherd of the

Sheep *at the last Day, I readily consented to this Publication; as also that all may see that we are in this, and in all other great Fundamentals of Religion, established in the same Faith with our Brethren, and all Sound and Orthodox Christians in the World: And cannot but look upon our selves greatly concerned, to see how Men by Craft and Subtlety endeavour, through Satan's Temptations (though I hope some do it not wittingly) strive to subvert the Gospel of Christ, and corrupt the Minds of weak Christians. An Error in a Fundamental Point, is dangerous and destructive; but should we mistake some Men we have do with, we should be glad: The Lord help you to stand fast in the Truth, as it is in Jesus (in which through Grace you are well established:) Our Days are perilous; Satan seems to be let loose upon us, and is in great Rage, his Time being but short. Brethren, 'tis a hard Case that any of those who maintain the Old Doctrine of Justification, should be branded with the black Name of Antinomians. As for my part, if Dr. Crisp be not misrepresented by his Opposers, I am not of the Opinion in several respects; but I had rather err on their side, who strive to exalt wholly the Free Grace of God, than on theirs, who seek to darken it and magnify the Power of the Creature, though we fear the Design is to wound the Truth and us, through that good Man's sides, who, I doubt not is come to heaven: O when shall we see that Truth, Peace, and Union longed for?*

My Brethren, the Doctrine we preach does not open a Door to the least Licentiousness: (as 'tis unjustly said to do by some, who are either willfully or ignorantly blind.)

No, God forbid. Nothing can promote Holiness, and Gospel-Sanctification like unto it, only it teaches us to act from high, sublime, and right Evangelical Principles: It shows the only way to attain to Gospel-Purity, flows from our Union with Christ, and that no Man can arrive to any degree of true Holiness, or expect to meet with any Success therein, without a Principle of Spiritual Life, or saving Faith in our Lord Jesus Christ. The Nature of Men must first be changed, and that Enmity that is in their Hearts against God, be removed, before they can be holy: The Tree must first be made good, or the Fruits will be evil. The Image of God must be formed in our Souls, which puts the Creature into an actual bent and propensity of his Heart to the Practice of Holiness. If a Man hates not Sin, be not out of Love with Sin, How should he be in love with God and Holiness? Now because we say Sanctification is not necessary, as antecedent to Justification, but is the Fruit or Product of Union with Christ; though we deny not but the Habits (of Holiness) are infused at that same Instant that Faith is wrought in the Soul, Must we be look'd upon as Promoters of a Licentious Doctrine? Must we make our own Performances, or Obedience a Condition of Justification, or be laid under infamy and Reproach? 'Tis by Faith only, that we come to have actual Enjoyment and Possession of Christ himself, and of Remission of Sin; and not only so, but of eternal Life; and so of Holiness also, and no other ways. The good Lord help you to a right Understanding of these things, and make you all a holy People, to the Praise of his Glory, and Honour of your Sacred Profession.

The Holy Apostle having asserted Justification by the Righteousness of God, which is by Faith in Jesus Christ, desired to know him and the Power of his Resurrection, etc. which he did not to be justified thereby, but as a Fruit flowing therefrom, or as a further Evidence thereof. The first he had attained; but there was a higher degree of Sanctification in his Eye, which he pressed after, as then not having attained: Whose Example let us follow.

I shall say no more: You own a Rule of Gospel-Holiness; Let me exhort you to labour after sincere Obedience: And pray forget me not in your Prayers, that God would graciously help me through all my Troubles and Temptations, and preserve me and you to his Heavenly Kingdom; who am your Servant for Jesus' sake, and so shall abide till Death.

Benjamin Keach

Biographical Preface
Benjamin Keach (1640-1704)

Benjamin Keach, a Particular Baptist minister of
Puritan persuasion, was born on February 29,
1640. His parents were unable to afford
schooling, so he was apprenticed as a tailor.
Nevertheless, Keach studied the Bible and
educated himself rigorously. Although baptized as
an infant, Keach came to Baptist convictions at a
young age, and was subsequently re-baptized at
age fifteen. Before long, be became distinguished
as one gifted for gospel ministry, and became a
non-ordained preacher at age eighteen in a
General Baptist church in Winslow,
Buckinghamshire. After the Restoration, Keach
was frequently arrested for his unlicensed
activities. In 1664, he scarcely escaped being
trampled on as soldiers interrupted one of his
meetings. He was saved by an officer's
intervention and subsequently imprisoned.

 Sometime in 1664 Keach published an
anonymous book, *The Child's Instructor*, which

attacked paedobaptism, endorsed lay preaching, and expressed millenarian convictions. The book was discovered by a local Anglican minister and Keach was brought to trial for sedition. He refused to renounce the book's tenets and so was imprisoned and pilloried. The pillory was designed as harsh punishment and consisted of the criminal being bound, head and arms, through a wood-like structure. Crowds were encouraged to throw items, which often caused permanent damage; the usual fare was vegetables, dead animals, and stones. But Keach used this occasion to preach before a supportive crowd. When Daniel Defoe was placed in the pillory at Charing Cross for writing a satire, public sympathy won out and the crowds threw flowers instead of stones. In both instances the purpose of the pillory was defeated. In Keach's case, however, public officials decided to execute the pillory more strictly and at Winslow, a week after his first pillory, Keach was humiliated with the burning of his book by the hangman. Of all the copies printed, some 1500, none survived. Keach was finally released and bound to good behavior.

Being unable to settle in Buckinghamshire, Keach preached in other counties on an itinerant basis from 1664 to 1668. During those years, he was imprisoned at least once more. He moved to London in 1668 and was ordained as an elder of a General Baptist congregation based in Tooley Street, Southwark. Being influenced there by William Kiffin and Hanserd

Knollys, Keach's theological convictions became increasingly Calvinistic.

A breach occurred in 1672 when Keach declared himself a Calvinist and he founded a Particular Baptist church in Horselydown, Southwark. After the declaration of indulgence, which allowed limited freedom for dissenting ministers, Keach facilitated a meeting house in Goat Street, Horselydown. The congregation grew rapidly in subsequent decades, and later came under the pastoral ministry of such famous pastors as John Gill and Charles Spurgeon.

Keach's subsequent years were marked by his involvement in various disputations, leadership among Particular Baptist churches, and pastoral labors among his flock. Concerning disputations, Keach entered into numerous debates against paedobaptists, Quakers, Seventh-Day Baptists, and even some among his own Particular Baptist circles, particularly through his promotion of hymn-singing, which he had advocated in his rewritten edition of *The Child's Instructor.* While he deviated from the characteristically Puritan doctrines of infant baptism and exclusive psalmody, he stood among other Puritans as a staunch defender for gospel truth against Richard Baxter's unorthodox views on justification. As a leader among Particular Baptists, he pushed for a ministry that had studied to show itself approved. By signing on to the Second London Confession of 1689, as well as his association with a Baptist catechism, Keach advocated a creedal tradition highly modeled after the Westminster Standards. As to his pastoral ministry, his experiential preaching and promotion of catechetical training which are markedly within the Puritan tradition, served to win many to Christ.

Keach's last years were spent ministering and publishing a variety of practical, theological, and seminal works (he seems to have run a printing and bookselling business from his house in Horsleydown). The most noted of these works are: *War with the Devil* (1673); *The Glorious Lover* (1679); *Tropologia: Or, A Key to Open Scripture Metaphors* (1681), his famous work on types and metaphors of the Bible, coauthored with Thomas Delaune—something modern reprints fail to mention; *The Travels of True Godliness* (1684), an allegory of similar vein to Bunyan's *Pilgrim's Progress*; *The Marrow of True Justification* (1692); *The Display of Glorious Grace* (1698), containing fourteen sermons on the covenant of grace; and *Spiritual Songs* (1700).

Keach died in London in 1704, and was buried in Southwark Park. According to relatives, Keach was a kind, gentle, and temperate man but was prone to outbursts of temper. He was said to be intolerant of alternative viewpoints and prone to single-mindedness, which, in some sense, was useful for establishing the Particular Baptists in the latter half of the seventeenth century.

Here are his major works that have been reprinted in recent years:

Exposition of the Parables (Kregel; 918 pages; 1974). Keach introduces this work with guidelines and principles for distinguishing parabolic passages in scripture, and explaining them effectively. He then embarks on 147 messages, covering forty-eight different passages from the gospels where our Lord makes use of similitude and parable in His teaching. Keach carefully determines the scope of each parable, draws out appropriate doctrines revealed, and makes fruitful application. This works provides great insight into preaching the parables, and remains a valuable resource for ministers to this day.

Preaching from the Types and Metaphors of the Bible (Kregel; 1034 pages; 1972). Originally published as *Tropologia: Or, A Key to Open Scripture Metaphors,* the first part of Keach's classic work distinguishes and describes the various figures of speech used in Scripture. By defining and demonstrating uses of such literary elements as metaphor, synecdoche, hyperbole, types, and parables, Keach helps his readers navigate through the vivid imagery of sacred Scripture. In the second part, he catalogues numerous elements of figurative language in Scripture, showing their proper significance and experimental value.

The Travels of True Godliness (Solid Ground; 210 pages; 2005). After defining godliness and showing its worthy pedigree and antiquity, "the excellent Benjamin Keach" (as he was fondly called), allegorically personifies "Godliness," much as Bunyan did "Christian." He introduces us to more than two dozen enemies of godliness, then details Godliness's encounters with several of them, including apostasy, hypocrisy, legalism, antinomianism, worldliness, and Satan. We meet in graphic detail the temptations of youth and old age, of riches and poverty, as well as the joys of contentment, thoughtfulness, kindness, and love. This is a fascinating read by the most important Baptist thinker of his day, designed to stir us up to a greater pursuit of godliness.

The Marrow of True Justification (Solid Ground, 96 pages, 2007). This work was first published in 1692, and makes for a great read still today both in addressing false teaching and in promoting the positive Reformation view of justification by faith alone in Jesus Christ and His imputed righteousness. This is one of the best works ever written on the subject. Here the central theme of the Christian gospel and the sure ground of the believer's hope is expounded with profound scriptural clarity. How the churches of today would benefit if pastors would preach this doctrine in contemporary dress as thoroughly, polemically, and winsomely as Keach did in his own day.

Dr. Joel R. Beeke
Grand Rapids, Michigan

THE
MARROW
OF
TRUE JUSTIFICATION:
OR,
The Doctrine of Justification opened,
in divers Sermons, at Horsly-down.

Rom. IV. 5
But to him that worketh not, but believeth on him that justifieth the Ungodly, his Faith is counted for righteousness.

THIS Text is given me (as I told you the last Lord's Day) by an unknown Hand, and though it may seem to interfere with my design and intention, in speaking to another Scripture, on a different subject; yet I readily embrace this Motion, and Answer the Desire of those Christian Friends, who so earnestly request and entreat me to speak to the Doctrine of Justification, and that for these Reasons following.

1. Because the Doctrine of Justification is one of the greatest and most weighty subjects I can insist upon; it being by all Christians acknowledged to be a Fundamental of Religion and Salvation. Hence this Article is justly styled, by worthy Writers, *Articulus stantis, vel cadentis Religionis: The very Pillar of the Christian Religion.* Other Subjects a Minister may Preach upon, and that unto the Profit and Advantage of the People; but this he must Preach, this he cannot omit, if he would truly Preach the Gospel of Jesus Christ.

2. Because I fear many Good Christians may not be so clearly and fully instructed into this Doctrine as they ought, or it might be wished they were, though they be rightly built upon the true Foundation, or upon that precious Cornerstone God hath laid in *Zion,* yet are but babes in Christ, and therefore need further Instruction, for their establishment in this, and other Essentials of the true Christian Religion.

3. Because the present Times are perilous, and many Grand Errors in and about this great Fundamental Point too much abound and prevail, (as many have with grief observed of late,) and that too in and about this City, which caused a worthy Minister lately to say, that it greatly concerned Pastors of the Churches, etc., to strive to establish their People in this Blessed Truth, since there are some who with all their Might endeavour to sow the Seeds of Error and Heresy almost every where, and many are sadly corrupted thereby already.

4. Because if a Person err herein, or be corrupt and of an unsound Faith, in the case of Justification, he is in a dangerous condition, though he may seem to be otherwise a Good Christian and of a Holy Life; for 'tis evident that there are damnable Principles, as well as damnable Practices, according to that in the Apostle *Peter, 2 Pet. 2.1,2.* And as our Saviour said to the *Jews, Unless ye believe that I am he, ye shall die in your Sins,* John 8.24. So must I say, Unless ye have a true and right Faith in him, *ye must die in your Sins;* for 'tis not enough to believe Christ is the true Saviour; but we must have also a right Faith in that Object; unbelief and misbelief are alike destructive and pernicious: Was it not an Error about Justification that caused the *Jews* to miscarry eternally, *viz. They being ignorant of Gods Righteousness, went about to establish their own Righteousness, etc.* Rom. 10.3.

5. Because this Doctrine tends so much to the Honour of God, and the magnifying of his infinite Wisdom, and his Free Grace, and Mercy in Jesus Christ, and also to the abasement of the Creature: Was it not the Exaltation of the Glory of God in all his Attributes and Blessed Perfections, which was the result of that Glorious Counsel, held above between the Father and the Son, before the World began, in the bringing in and establishment of the Covenant of Grace? What did God, as I may say, design or aim at therein, more that his own Glory, and to abase sinful Man? And if so, how doth it behoove us to see to our utmost to open the Channel, that this Sovereign Grace may run freely,

and not be obstructed by the Mud or cursed Notions and Errors of Men's dark Minds, who seek to Eclipse the Doctrine of God's Free Grace?

6. Because from this Doctrine doth proceed all the Hope we have of Eternal Life: Destroy this Foundation, and what can the righteous do? I may say of Justification through the imputation of Christ's righteousness, as *David* speaks of the Covenant of Grace, *This is all our Salvation and our Hope, etc. 2 Sam. 23.5.* If we come not to Heaven this way, I know no other; *for other Foundation can no Man lay, than that is laid, which is Jesus Christ,* 1 Cor. 3.11.

7. Because 'tis a Doctrine that affords so much sweet and Divine Comfort to our Souls, when rightly understood and apprehended; and I am persuaded 'tis through the want of Light, and clear knowledge of this Doctrine, so many Doubts and Fears attend many Good Christians: For (as I have told some of you lately), divers weak Saints are ready to judge of their Justification according to the degree and measure of their Sanctification; and can hardly be brought to believe, such vile Creatures as they are, who find such evil and deceitful Hearts, and so many great Evils and infirmities in their Lives, can be Justified in the sight of God; (not that I ever denied that Sanctification and Holiness, is a Mark or Evidence of a Justified Person;) though I deny Justification to be a gradual Act, as Sanctification in us is; or that a Person is not perfectly Justified until he is perfectly Sanctified, or actually delivered in himself from the pollution and

defilement of all Sin; for then it would follow, No Believer is actually Justified in this Life: But that which I intend, and hint at, is this, That if some weak Christians can but arrive to Holy and Spiritual Frames in Duty, and get power over their Corruptions, then they think they have good grounds to believe and hope they may be Justified; as if it were inherent Grace and Holiness that Justifies them in God's sight.

So much, briefly, as to the Grounds and Reasons which induced me to Answer the Call I had to insist upon this Text and Subject.

Secondly, To proceed the more orderly, I shall give you the scope and coherence of the Text itself, for the better understanding the design and main drift of the Holy Ghost therein.

And as to this we need go no further back than to the 9 verse of the 3 Chap. where the Apostle proves, that all Men, both Jews and Gentiles, are under Sin: *What then are we better than they? No, in no wise; for we have before proved, both Jews and Gentiles, that they are all under Sin, verse 9.* This he confirms by the Scriptures of the Old Testament; particularly, by that of *David, There is none righteous no not one,* verse 10. All Men, naturally, as considered under the Fall, are ungodly and vile in the sight of God; and although the *Jews* thought themselves in a better condition than the Gentiles were, and boasted of their Knowledge and Sanctity; the Apostle declares, they were not withstanding abominable Sinners, and in no better State, but deceived themselves; and that he might make this farther manifest, he proceeds more particularly to discover their wretched Pollution and Filthiness: *There is none that understandeth*, verse 11.

1. He shows that all the Faculties of the Soul are corrupted, *viz.* their Minds and Understandings are blind and darkened, being ignorant of God, or without the knowledge of his pure and spotless Nature, Justice, and Holiness: *There is none that seeketh after God.*

2. By this he shows also the Poison and Venom that was got into the Will; for as they have lost God, so they will not seek after him, like that of our Saviour, *Ye will not come to me that you might have Life*, John 5. 40. Now till a Man comes to see his own wretched and woeful condition, and understands the Nature of God, and the Nature and Tenure of the Holy Law of God, he cannot discern that absolute necessity there is of a perfect and complete righteousness to Justify him in God's sight.

3. And that their Will and Affections are also depraved, and like manner corrupted, he proceeds farther to cite what *David* in the same Psalm saith, viz. *They are all gone out of the way, they are altogether become unprofitable, there is none that doth good, no not one*, verse 12.

Now lest any one Zealot should fancy himself in a good condition, and excluded from this black indictment, and so in a Justified State, by his own righteousness, he confirms again his former Universal Charge, *All are gone out of the way, they are altogether become unprofitable*, and therefore not one of them can be justified.

And as the Faculties of their Souls are corrupt, so the Apostle proceeds to show the infection had seized on the Members of their Bodies; therefore he saith, *Their Throat is an open Sepulcher, with their Tongue they have used Deceit, the Poison of Asps is under their Lips*, verse 13. *Whose Mouth is full of cursing and bitterness*, verse 14. *Their Feet are swift to shed Blood*, verse 15. Both Tongues, Lips, Throats, and Feet, are polluted and abominable, being Instruments of unrighteousness.

In verse 19, he seems to Answer, by way of anticipation, an Objection, which the Jews might bring against what he had said, as if they should say, What you speak doth not concern us, but the profane Gentiles; we have the Law, and that relieves us, and thereby we may be Justified; to which he Reasons thus, to cut off all their Hopes, *viz. Now we know that whatsoever the Law saith, it saith unto them that are under the Law, that ever Mouth may be stopped, and all the World become guilty before God.*

1. By the Law is not only meant the Law as it was given to *Israel* in the Two Tables of Stone, but as the substance of the same Law was written in the Hearts of all Mankind; the Apostle means the Law of the First Covenant, which was broken by our First parents, by the breach of which all the World became guilty before God originally; and also by their actual Breach thereof; for that neither Jews nor Gentiles lived without Sin: but contrariwise were guilty of the Breach of that Law, under which

they lived: But although all the World were under the Law of the First Covenant, and had the same Law as to the substance of it, as a rule of Life; yet the *Jews* had the upper hand of the rest of the World, by their having the Oracles of God committed to them, by which means they had greater advantages to come to the knowledge of Sin, and also by means of divers Figures and Prophecies to the knowledge of the *Messiah*.

But what of all this? the Apostle shows them that the Law on which they rested, was so far from relieving them, that it served chiefly to convince them of their horrid guilt, and bound the Sentence upon them, so that they and all the World were subject to the Just Judgment of God, and under his Wrath and Curse.

2. And therefore he infers, that by the Law (either as it was written in the Two Tables, or in the Heart, which the *Gentiles* had as well as the *Jews*) no Man could be justified so, *ver. 20. Therefore by the deeds of the Law shall no flesh be justified in his sight, for by the Law is the knowledge of Sin.*

3. But lest upon this, the lost World should be left under utter Despair, the Apostle proceeds to show us there is a way found out in the infinite Wisdom of God, and according to his unspeakable Grace and Goodness, to deliver us from Sin and Guilt, and so to justify us before God; and therefore he adds, *but now the Righteousness of God without the Law is manifested, being witnessed by the Law and the Prophets, v. 21. Even the Righteousness of God, which is by faith of Jesus Christ unto all, and upon all that*

believe; for there is no difference, v. 22. For all have sinned, and come short of the glory of God, being justified freely by his Grace, through the Redemption that is in Jesus Christ, v. 23, 24.

No wonder there is no difference, when both *Jews* and *Gentiles* lie under the guilt of *Adam's* Transgression, it being imputed to them, he being the common Head and Representative of the whole race of Mankind, *Rom. 5. 12.* And since also all of them partake of the same original Corruption or depraved Nature, inherent in them, from whence proceed all those actual Transgressions, by which means it appears that all come short of that glorious Image of God, in which they were at first created; and also of the eternal Glory above: Yet to the praise of God's Grace, the lost World is not left in a hopeless Condition, God having sent his Son to satisfy the Law and Divine Justice, or to *be a propitiation through Faith in his Blood, to declare his Righteousness for the remission of Sins that are past, through the forbearance of God,* v. 25.

4. In the 27th Verse, he adds, a God-honoring, and a self-confounding Inference from what he had said, *Where is boasting then? It is excluded, by what Law? Of Works? Nay, but by the Law of Faith.*

5. And hence he draws another conclusion, *viz. ver. 28. Therefore we conclude, That a man is justified by faith without the works of the Law,* and in the 4th Chapter he proceeds to prove his main Argument; *i.e.* That a Sinner is justified by Faith without Works, by the Example of *Abraham, for if Abraham*

*were justified by works, he hath whereof to glory, but not
before God,* chap. 4. 2.

6. This is the Apostle's Argument: if *Abraham*
was justified by Works, he had somewhat whereby
he might boast and glory; but *Abraham* had nothing
whereof to boast or glory; and therefore he was not
justified by Works.

But to put it further out of doubt, he affirms
what the Scripture saith; *viz.* That *Abraham believed
God, and it was counted to him for Righteousness,* v. 3.

7. In the next place, he proceeds to prove his
blessed Doctrine from the nature of Works and
Grace, they being quite opposite, and contrary the
one to the other. *Now to him that worketh, is the
reward not reckoned of grace but of debt,* v. 4. If therefore
it was granted, a Man could perform the condition
of perfect Obedience, yet he could not be justified.

1. Because all, (as he had showed before,) have
sinned.

2. Because there is no Reward as a due debt
from God, because we can do no more than our
Duty, we being the Lords, and all our Abilities and
Services can ne'er make a reparation for the wrong
we have done against the Law, and the Holiness,
and Justice of God.

And thus I come to my Text, *ver.* 5.

*But to him that worketh not, but believeth on him that
justifieth the ungodly, his faith is counted for Righteousness.*

To him that worketh not; That is, worketh not,
thinking thereby to be justified and saved. Though
he may work, *i.e.* lead a holy and righteous Life; yet

he doth it not to merit thereby; nay, though he be wicked, and an ungodly person, and so worketh not, or hath no Moral Righteousness at all; yet if he *believeth on him that justifieth the ungodly, his faith is counted* or imputed *for righteousness;* Not as a simple Act, or as it is a quality or habit, or in us, as the Papists teach; *ipsa fides,* saith *Bellarmine, censetur esse Justitia,* Faith itself is counted to be a Justice, and itself is imputed unto Righteousness; No, nor in respect of the effects or fruits of it; for so it is part of our Sanctification.

But as it is a hand to take hold of, or receive, or apply Christ and his Righteousness.

Manus accipientis, saith Dr. *Downham,* the hand of the Receiver is the Grace of justifying Faith: 'Tis not Faith, but the Object and Righteousness Faith apprehends or takes hold of, that *justifies the ungodly.*

The Apostle doth not intend by these Words, That if a Man hath the Works here meant, he cannot be justified, unless he throws them away, and become openly wicked and profane; and so sin that Grace may abound; No, as the Apostle says, *God forbid,* Rom. 6.1. But his meaning is, that the absence or want of good Works, or moral Righteousness, cannot hinder a Man's justification, if he believes in Jesus Christ, though he be never so wicked and ungodly.

That justifieth the ungodly. Every Man is ungodly before he is acquitted and justified, having till that very instant a great Mountain of guilt and filth lying upon him.

Justifie; tis *Verbum forense,* a judicial Word, used in Courts of Judgment, or a Law Term, which usually is opposed to Condemnation.   And it signifies to absolve, to acquit from guilt, and accepting a Man as righteous, or to pronounce him just and righteous, or give sentence for him, *Deut.* 25.1., *Prov.* 17.15. *not* the making a person inherently righteous; but to count or impute Righteousness to one, that is in himself a Sinner, or as my Text, *ungodly.*

Obj. But may be you will say, what ungodly ones doth God justify: if it be an impenitent, ungodly one, how can you reconcile this Text with that of *Solomon, He that justifieth the wicked, and he that condemneth the just, even they are both abomination to the Lord?* Prov. 17.15.

1. Answ. I answer; 'tis not meant of justifying of any ungodly Act of a wicked Person; for God can as soon cease to be, as to justify the ungodly.

2. Nor Secondly, he means not justifying the person in his committing of any sinful deed; for that is as opposite to God's holy Nature, and all one with the former.

3. Nor in the Negative, are they such ungodly ones that are righteous in their own Eyes, like as many of the *Jews* and *Pharisees* were, and *Paul* also before his Conversion, *Phil.* 3.4,5,6,7, when a Persecutor.

For although such who are Righteous in their own sight, are the worst of Sinners in the sight of God; yet they are such whom God, while they retain that conceit of themselves, will never justify:

Christ *did not come to call the righteous, but sinners to Repentance. There is*, saith *Solomon, a Generation pure in their own eyes, yet are they not cleansed from their filthiness*, Prov. 30.12. Our Saviour compares this sort of Men to *painted Sepulchers, who appear beautiful without, but are within full of dead Men's bones, and of all uncleanness*, Matt. 23.27.

What pollution is more loathsome than the filth of a rotten and stinking Sepulcher? The proud *Pharisee* cries out, *God, I thank thee I am not as other Men are, Extortioners, Unjust, Adulterers, or even as this Publican. I fast twice in the week, I give Tithes of all that I possess*, Luke 18.11,12. These Men boast of their good Works, Prayers, and Alms-deeds; but never saw their horrid Pride, hardness of their hearts, Unbelief, and cursed Hypocrisy; They *make clean the outside of the cup and platter;* but are abominable inwardly in his eye who beholds their hearts. These Men are wicked and ungodly, notwithstanding they look upon themselves to be Righteous; and yet are not therefore the ungodly whom God will justify. 'Tis said, *the Publican who cried, Lord be merciful to me a Sinner, went away rather justified,* than the proud *Pharisee*, Luke 18:13,14.

4. And in the fourth place, neither are they such wicked and ungodly ones, who though openly profane and wretched Creatures, such that love, and live in Sin; yet glory presumptuously of Christ's Death, and say, through him they hope to be saved: They believe in Christ; and therefore do not doubt of their Salvation; Faith is one thing, and Presumption is another. I am afraid, Brethren, that

this conceit and delusion of the Devil sends daily many thousands to Hell; because God hath abounded in his Grace, they abound in Sin and Wickedness, and presumptuously trust to lying Words: These ungodly ones are not the persons which God doth justify; but rather positively condemns in his Word, and will condemn for ever, unless they believe, truly believe in Jesus Christ.

5. Therefore in the Fifth place, they are such ungodly ones in the Affirmative, who do see themselves to be ungodly and vile; they are such, whom God brings to see their Sickness, to feel themselves wounded, who find themselves lost and undone; nay, though some of them may like *Paul* be blameless, in respect of the outward Acts of Sin; yet by *the coming of the Commandment with powerful Conviction, sin revives and they die*, Rom. 7. They see the pollution of their Hearts, and the depravity of their nature, and behold themselves the worst of Men.

Though some others may be indeed guilty of gross Acts of Sin, or notorious Transgressors, even just until that very instant that they hear the Gospel preached, and have done no Acts of Righteousness; yet if they believe on Jesus Christ, or throw themselves by an Act of saving Faith on the Blood and Merits of Christ, they are immediately justified; for let Men have moral Righteousness, or no moral Righteousness, they are all ungodly in God's sight, till they believe; and at that very instant they do believe, they are accounted righteous through the Imputation of Christ's perfect Righteousness: For as a Man's own Righteousness cannot further his Justification, or conduce or add thereto; so his Sin and Ungodliness cannot hinder or obstruct his Justification, if he truly believe on him who justifies the Ungodly.

My Brethren, do not mistake; a Man seeing himself wounded doth not heal him, though it may, and does put him upon seeking out for healing, so a Man seeing himself a Sinner, doth not render him Righteous. Nothing renders a Man righteous to Justification in God's sight, but the Imputation of the perfect Personal Righteousness of Christ, received only by the Faith *of the Operation of God.* When I was a Lad, I was greatly taken with a Book, called *The flowing of Christ's Blood freely to Sinners, as Sinners.* O, my Brethren, that's the Case, that's the Doctrine which the Apostle preaches; you must come to Christ, believe on Christ, as Sinners, as Ungodly ones, and not as Righteous, not as Saints, and Holy persons, *The whole need not a Physician, but they that are sick.* The Thief on the Cross, as a Sinner, cry'd out, *Lord remember me, &c.* and the Jailor as a Sinner, cry'd out, *Sirs, what must I do to be saved?* So much as to the Explanation of the Terms of the Text; in which you have three parts:

1. A Negative Proposition, *But to him that worketh not.*
2. An Affirmative Proposition, *But believeth on him that justifies the ungodly.*
3. The Conclusion from hence, *His faith is counted (or imputed) for Righteousness.*

The Observations I shall take notice of from the Words, shall be but two.

1. *Doct. That all Works done by the Creature, are quite excluded in point of Justification of a Sinner in the sight of God.*
2. *That Justification is wholly of the free Grace of God, through the Imputation of the perfect Righteousness of Jesus Christ by Faith.*

I purpose to begin with the first of these Points of Doctrine, and then come to speak to the second. But before I proceed, I shall show you divers false and erroneous Principles, which men have sucked in, in and about the great Doctrine of Justification.

I shall then prove the Point, *viz.* That all Works done by the Creature are quite excluded in point of justification of a Sinner in God's sight.

1. I shall begin with the *Papists,* who hold that Men are Justified by inherent Righteousness, by Good Works, and not by Faith only, affirming Good Works to be meritorious, or that Men thereby deserve Eternal Life; nay, that a Man may perfectly fulfill the Law of God, though he cannot live without Sin: But to men the matter, *Bellarmine's* Argument is, That Venial Sins, of which he denies not, that all are guilty; yet they do not hinder a Man from keeping the Law perfectly; The foolishness of which distinction is easily discerned; for if they be Sins which he calls Venial, then they are the Transgression of the Law, and he that transgresses the Law doth not keep it perfectly, but contrariwise breaks it, and so is accursed, cast, and condemned by it: But they affirm, that a Man may not only, by his Good Works, merit for himself; but also may do more than is commanded, or may do Works of Supererogation, or do more than his Duty.

2. The second sort I shall mention are the *Socinians*, who deny the Deity of the Son of God; and from hence deny also the Satisfaction of Christ, because the latter depends upon the former: it was from the dignity and excellency of Christ's Person, he being God as well as Man, that his Sacrifice had such infinite value and worth in it, that by one single payment (as I may so say) he made such a full compensation to the Law and Justice of God: But they erring in those two grand Points of Christian Religion, run into the third, and deny the imputation of Christ's Personal righteousness to us in Justification. And indeed it seems to me that this sort of Men assert that Justification of the Sinner, is nothing more than God's pardoning him freely by his Mercy, and that only as a simple act of his own Mercy and Grace, without respect had to the Satisfaction made for our Sins by Jesus Christ, by which act of God's pardoning Grace they affirm the guilt of Sin that binds the Sinner over to punishment is taken off, and so he is acquitted and delivered from Eternal Wrath; but could this be admitted which they affirm why should God send his beloved Son into the World to be a Sacrifice for Sin? For could not God, without that Glorious Fruit of his infinite Goodness, have pardoned and

acquitted us, and never have suffered his Son to have undergone such pain and sorrow for us, which indeed he did?

3. Another sort there be, which are those called *Arminians*, of which there are many of late Times.

I find one of them does affirm, *That though the Works of the Law are excluded from justifying the Sinner in the sight of God; yet Gospel Works are not;* So that they include Love to God, Acts of Mercy, and other Gospel Duties, and Obedience in point of Justification, as well as Faith, or join Good Works done under the Gospel and Faith together; and this plainly appears by what Mr. *William Allen* hath wrote in his Book, called, *A Glass Of Justification*, or *the Work of Faith with Power*, See p. 18. These are his Words, *viz. It is no where, neither in Words nor Sense, said, but he that loveth not, but believeth on him that Justifieth the Ungodly, his Faith, is counted to him for righteousness.* Sure this Man forgot that Love to God was one great thing the Law commanded: Were not the *Israelites*, or the People of the *Jews*, under the Law, to do all they did in Love to God? *Thou shalt Love the Lord thy God, with all they Heart, and with all thy Soul, and with all thy strength, &c.* He proceeds to blame our Protestant Writers, in asserting Justification by Faith alone, without Works. Brethren, although we do not oppose Faith to Love; as if Faith, that is of the right Kind, can be without Love to God; yet we say, 'tis Faith and not Works; not Love, nor Deeds of Mercy, nor any other Gospel Duties, or Obedience, that is *counted to us for righteousness.* And why to Faith only? Because that Grace only carries us out of our selves to another for righteousness, *i.e.* to Jesus Christ.

4. The same sort affirm Faith doth Justify the Sinner (as far as I can gather) as it is the act of the Creature, God accepting of that internal act of the Soul, according to his good pleasure, to Justification; not having respect so to the Object of Faith, as that the matter thereof is Christ, perfect righteousness, and the form or formal Cause of it, the Imputation thereof, to such who believe in Jesus, but that it hath pleased God to appoint or ordain Faith, in respect of itself, to that end and purpose; namely, to Justify the Sinner.

Of this sort are the *Dutch Arminians*, in pursuance of their main Doctrine of Free Will; they exalt Man's Works, and therefore affirm, that he is Justified, not by Christ's righteousness, but by his own Faith; God having required of him, instead of full Obedience to the Law of Works, that now he should believe on his Son; and that for so doing he should be Justified and saved, as he should have been before for perfect Obedience: So that with this sort (as one observes) *Faith* is that righteousness for which we are Justified before God. Moreover, they tell us, that Faith is a belief of the Truth of the Gospel, so as to live according to it; thus it includeth, and not excludeth Works; and that Faith and Works, or Obedience to the Gospel, is our righteousness for which we are Justified and saved. At the same time you must remember that they do not own Faith to be the Gift of God, or a Grace of the Holy Spirit; but that which the

Creature has power, when the Gospel is Preached, to act by common assistance, and influences, he hath power to do, and perform as any other Duties of Religion, as to *Pray, hear the Word, &c. And thus* they make the whole stress of Man's Salvation (after all that Christ hath done) to depend upon the depraved and corrupt Will of the Creature; and saith, such a condition of Justification and Eternal Life, as may or may not be performed, which, if true, it might so fall out, that not one Soul might be saved, notwithstanding the precious price paid by Jesus Christ to redeem them; for by the same purity of Reason one Man may resist the offers of Grace, and not believe in Christ, or exert that power, every Man may as well do so too. See Mr. *John Troughton's Lutherus Redivivus*, p.2.

5. Some also there be, who affirm, that Justification consisteth in our being perfectly and inherently Holy, by the Spirit, Light, or Christ within; and that no Man can be Justified, unless he be in himself perfect without Sin. These Men, for all their late pretences, in talking of Christ's righteousness; yet 'tis evident those who assert this Doctrine say, *God doth not accept any, where there is any failing, or do not fulfill the Law, and Answer every demand of Justice*, Edw. Burroughs *Works*, 14 *Queries, p. 33.* And another of their chief Teachers saith, *That Justification by the righteousness of another, or which Christ fulfilled for us, in his own Person, wholly without us, we boldly affirm* (saith he, *to be a Doctrine of Devils, and an Arm of the Sea of Corruption, which doth now Deluge the World,* Wm. Pen's *Apol. p. 143.* And again he says,

It is a great Abomination to say God should condemn and punish his innocent Son, that he having satisfied for our Sins we may be justified by the imputation of his perfect righteousness, Pen's *Sandy foundation, p. 25.* And then afterwards speaking of that Text, Rom. 2.13. *Not the Hearers of the Law are Just before God, but the Doers of it shall be Justified. From whence,* saith he, *how unanswerably may I observe, that unless we become Doers of that Law which Christ came not to destroy, but as our Example to fulfill, we cannot be Justified before God? Nor let any fancy that Christ hath fulfilled it for them, as to exclude their Obedience from being required to their Acceptance, but only as their Pattern,* Pen's *Sandy Foundation, p. 26.* No marvel they Preach up a sinless Perfection to be attainable in this Life, or that Men may live and not Sin at all, since without an actual Obedience in our own Persons to the Law in every part and branch of it, no Man can be Justified in the sight of God. We say there is no Man can be Justified, but by a complete and perfect righteousness, either inherent in us, or imputed to us; but 'tis evident, by what I have already showed, no Man hath such a righteousness in himself; there being *none that doth good, and sinneth not; if we say we have no Sin, we deceive ourselves, and the Truth is not in us, 1 John 1.8. Paul* cried out, *When he would do Good, Sin was present with him,* Rom. 7. Besides, if a Man could live and Sin not, yet he could not thereby be Justified, because all have sinned, and broke God's Law, who shall therefore satisfy for, and pay off the old score.

6. Another sort there be, that hold, that some things must be done by the Creature, not only to prepare for, but to procure Justification, not believing they can have this *Wine and Milk, without Money and without price*, Isa. 55.1,2. or something of their own.

They think they must make themselves clean, and then come to Christ to be washed, and Justified.

7. There are others of late, as well as formerly, who by too many are looked upon to be true Preachers of the Gospel, and Orthodox Men, who are strangely tainted with that poisonous Notion, which brings in sincere Obedience unto the Gospel, as joining it with Faith in point of Justification. Thus I find they express themselves, *viz.* That Faith and Obedience are Conditions of the Gospel, or of the Covenant of Grace, as perfect Obedience was of the Covenant of Works; and that Christ hath purchased by his Death, that this new Covenant should be made with us, *viz.* That if we would believe and obey the Gospel, we should be pardoned and saved, *&c.* Therefore that for which we are Justified and saved, is our Faith and Obedience, and so far as I can gather, the Faith they speak of doth not respect the taking hold of Christ's Righteousness, *&c.* but the Belief of the acceptance of our Person's Holiness, and sincere Obedience to the Gospel, through Christ, to our Justification; Christ having taken away, by his Death, the rigor of the Law of the First Covenant, which required perfect Righteousness in point of

Justification, and hath made the terms of our Justification easier, *viz.* instead of perfect Obedience, God will now accept of imperfect Obedience, if sincere, and acquit us from Condemnation, and receive us to Eternal Life.

Now such, who have always been looked upon as sound in this great Fundamental Point of Justification, believe and teach, *Christ came not to destroy the Law, but to fulfill it,* and in our nature, and stead as our Head Representative and Surety, to do and perform the terms thereof; I mean the Law of Works, which we had broken and by his Death made a full compensation to the Justice of God for our breach of it, whose Actual and Passive Obedience, or Righteousness, is imputed to all who believe in him.

We say Obedience supposeth a Man Justified; but these Men say, that Obedience concurs with Faith to Justify, or is part of our righteousness to Justification: We affirm, as a Worthy Divine Observes, that Faith alone perfectly Justifies, by trusting in the Righteousness of Christ, so that *there is no Condemnation to them who are in Jesus Christ,* Rom. 8.1. or truly believe in him; but they teach that Faith and Obedience Justify only, as the Conditions of the Gospel, *i.e.* as thereby we doing what the Gospel requires of us; and so we are Justified, or accepted, so far as our Faith and Obedience go, and no farther; and when they are perfect at Judgment, we shall be perfectly Justified; so that they render our Justification to be as imperfect as our inherent Personal Holiness or Sanctification is imperfect; or to give it in the Words of a Learned Writer, they intimate, while we are imperfect our Justification is imperfect also; and if our Faith and Obedience be interrupted or utterly lost, Justification is interrupted and utterly lost likewise; nor is it any wonder our Justification should be look'd upon by them to be imperfect, while any Imperfections remain in us, if the perfect Righteousness of Christ, be not the matter of our Justification, or that which does Justify us in God's sight; and on the other Hand 'tis impossible, if we are Justified and accepted as just Persons, and graciously acquitted by the Righteousness of Christ, there should be the least stain, imperfection, or spot, in our Justification; but that Christ must needs say of such, in respect of Justification, as he doth of his Spouse, *Thou are all fair, my Love, and there is not spot in thee,* Cant. 4.7. And how should it be otherwise, since there was no spot nor blemish found in him.

Mr. *Baxter,* in his Fourth Proposition, in his Preface to D. *Tully,* saith, that this Condition (*viz.* the Covenant of Grace, by which we have right to the benefits of it) is our Faith [mark it] or Christianity, as it is meant by Christ in the Baptismal Covenant, *viz.* to give up our selves in Covenant, believing, in God the Father, Son, and Holy Ghost, renouncing the contraries; and that though this consent to the Christian Covenant (called Faith alone) be the full Condition of our Right to the Benefit of that Covenant (of which Justification is one,) yet obediential Performances, and Conquest of Temptations, and Perseverance, are secondary parts of the Condition of our Right, as continued and consummated; he saith for Faith to be *imputed to us for righteousness, Rom. 4.22,23,24.* is plainly meant, that God, who under the Law of innocency required perfect Obedience of us to Justification and Glorification, upon the Satisfaction and Merits of Christ, hath freely given a full Pardon and Right to Life to all true Believers; so that now by the Covenant of Grace, nothing is required of us to our Justification, but Faith, all the rest being done by Christ; and so Faith in God the Father, Son, and Holy Ghost, is reputed truly to be the condition on our part, on which Christ and Life by that Baptismal Covenant is made ours.

Observe, here is not a Word concerning Christ's Righteousness or Faith in him for Righteousness. And hence worthy Mr. *Troughton* citing this passage of Mr. 'Baxter saith, By this Author, 'tis not Christ's Righteousness apprehended by Faith, 'justifieth us; but Faith itself, as including Obedience, *i.e.* the belief and practice of 'the Christian Religion is our Righteousness, by, and for which we are justified and 'accepted, *Luth. Rd. p. 8.*

Moreover, 'tis worth noting to observe how Mr. *Baxter* seems to lay the whole stress of our first Justification to what is promised in our Baptismal Covenant, wherein we profess Faith in God the Father, Son, and Holy Ghost; sure he might with much ease have foreseen that such who entered into that Baptismal Covenant in the Primitive, Apostolical Days, were such who before they were admitted thereto, were required to believe: And if true Subjects were all justified before they sign'd that Covenant, the Jailor who cried out, *Sirs, what must I do to be saved*, was by St. *Paul* required *to believe on the Lord Jesus*, with a Promise upon his so doing of being saved. Though I deny not, but that Faith in God the Father, and in the Holy Ghost, is enjoined as well as Faith in the Son; yet 'tis Christ who is the immediate Object of our Faith, and that too as he was crucified for us, and bore our Sins, or *was made sin for us, that we might be made the righteousness of God in him*. And 'tis by him that we come to God, and believe in God, and are justified and accepted of God, *other foundation* (of these things) *can no man lay*. But Mr. *Baxter* speaks nothing of this, but of a Faith in general in God the Father, Son, and Holy Ghost, which Faith he says is reputed truly to be the Condition on our part on which Christ and Life by that Baptismal Covenant is made ours.

Till I met with this passage of Mr. *Baxter's*, I did not so well understand what Mr. *Daniel Williams* means by those Assertions of his in his late Book, called *The Vanity of Youth*, p. 130, 131. who answers these Questions following, *viz.*

What doth the Covenant bind thee to? (meaning the Baptismal Covenant)

Answ. *To be the Lords in a sincere Care to know, love, believe, obey, work and serve him all my days, and to depend on God through Christ for all Happiness*, Ezek. 16.8. Rom. 12.1. Rom. 6.4.

Quest. *What if a Child through the love of Sin, or vanity of Mind, will not agree to this Covenant when he is capable?*

Answ. *He then rejecteth Christ the Saviour, and renounceth the Blessings of the Gospel.*

Quest. *Is it a great Sin to refuse to agree to the Covenant to which thy Baptism engaged thee?*

Answ. *It's the damning Sin, and the heart of all Sin.*

I suppose Mr. *Williams*, and Mr. *Baxter* were of the same Faith and Judgment. If you will know that the Terms and Condition of the Covenant of Grace are, which must be performed by us that we may be justified, both these Men tell you, (though the latter more fully) 'tis to make good this Baptismal Covenant, *viz.* sincerely to love, obey, worship, and serve the Lord; so that Faith alone as it receives Christ, or helps us to fly to Christ, and rely on Christ, is not the alone way or condition (if it may be so termed) on our part in order to actual Interest in Jesus Christ, and Justification; but also the whole of Gospel-Obedience and Holiness, they make to be as Absolute Conditions in order thereunto, as Faith. Sirs, we deny not but that Obedience and Personal Holiness is necessary to Salvation, or in order to a meetness for an actual Possession of Heaven: But we must exclude all inherent Holiness or Works of Obedience done by us, in point of Justification. Pray mind my Text, *But to him that worketh not, but believeth.*

But if it be not as I affirm concerning these Men, how can Mr. *Williams* call the *non*-performance of the Baptismal Covenant, *the damning Sin, and heart of all Sin.*

Observe the very same damning Evil, which the Holy Ghost charges on the Sin of Unbelief. In the New Testament, *Mark 16.16. John 3.36.* he charges on the *non*-performance of his new Condition of Justification, and Eternal Life; *i.e.* this Baptismal Covenant: All Sin (I grant) is damning in its own Nature, every Sin being a breach of God's Law, exposes to God's Wrath and Curse: But the not agreeing to, or *non*-performance of this Covenant (the making this the Condition of the Covenant of Grace) he calls, by way of Eminency, *the damning Sin*, and heart of all Sin.   If this Man preaches Christ, or the glorious Gospel, I am much mistaken.

Besides, our Baptismal Covenant is not a sign of that Faith and Holiness we Could afterwards obtain; but 'tis an outward sign of that inward Grace we have (or ought to have when baptized) *i.e.* 'tis a sign that we are dead to Sin, to the World, to the Law, and to our own Righteousness: *How shall we* (saith the Apostle) *who are dead to Sin, live any longer therein,* Rom. 6.4. *Know ye not, that so many of us as were baptized into Jesus Christ, were baptized into his death,* v. 3. *Therefore we are buried with him by Baptism into Death; that like as Christ was raised up from the dead by the glory of the Father, so we should walk in newness of Life.*

These Persons who were baptized, being true Believers, were in a justified State; and though tis true, they by their Baptismal Covenant promised to walk in newness of Life; yet the neglect of this is nowhere called the damning Sin; nor is the performance of it that Righteousness they desire to be found in to Justification. But tis evident, these Men place Obedience and Personal Holiness in the place of Faith, and the *non*-performance of that inherent Holiness and Obedience in the room of unbelief; though we grant without Holiness no Man shall ever see the Lord; yet 'tis not for that, or thereby we are justified, and shall be saved, but by the Personal Righteousness of Jesus Christ.

But to proceed as a further Confirmation, that these Men deny that the Righteousness of Christ, as 'tis apprehended or received by Faith, is that alone through which we are justified, I might here cite another Author, Mr. *Truman, Grand Propitiation*, p. 30. 86. who paraphrasing on those Words, *Rom. 3.26. That he might be just, and the Justifier of him that believeth in Jesus.* He saith, That he that is of the Faith of Jesus, or of the Christian Faith, τῆς ἐπιπιςτὰς Ἰηςοῦ; And concerning the Effects of the Death of Christ, or his Satisfaction, he saith, It was only this, that the Obstacle being removed (*viz.* offended Justice) God might be at liberty to act in the pardon of Sinners, in what way and upon what Terms he pleased. The immediate Effect is that God might be just, though he should pardon Sinners, that he might pardon *Salva Justitia*, not, that he must pardon, come what will of it, or be unjust. And further, to exclude Christ's Righteousness from being the Matter of our Justification, (saith Mr. *Troughton*) he saith, that in our Redemption, we 1. are not properly to be looked upon as Debtors, nor God properly as a Creditor, but as a Governor and Legislator, we as Subjects, and that Christ acted not the part of a Surety (though he be once figuratively so called) but of a Mediator expiating Guilt, and making reparation to Justice some other way than by the Execution of the Law; yea, endeavoring that the legal threat might not be executed by making amends, for the *non*-execution of it. 2. The Sufferings of Christ were not properly an Execution of the Law (though they may figuratively be so called) but a Satisfaction to Justice. And further, that it is contrary to Scripture and Reason, to hold that Christ's fulfilling of, and Obedience to the Law is accounted imputed, as if believers had fulfilled and obeyed the Law in his doing it.

1. And thus these Men go about to shake, if they could, nay, overthrow the great Article of our Faith, and glorious Doctrine of Justification, as it hath been generally received by all Orthodox Christians in every Age of the Church clearly denying that which Christ did and suffered, he did and suffered as a common Person, as a Head, Surety and Representative for all the Elect; but that he did all merely as a Mediator, *viz.* As one endeavoring to compose the difference betwixt God and Sinners.

2. Not that he fulfilled the Law of Works for us in our stead; but that he fulfilled the peculiar Law of a Mediator.

3. Not that Christ by undergoing the Curse of the Law delivered Mankind from the Curse thereof; and by his active Obedience unto the Precepts of it,

purchased Life for them, which the Law promised with other super-abounding additional Blessings; but rather give Man a new and a milder Law of Grace or Terms of Life, according as the Father and the Son should, or did agree. And only gave to God a valuable Consideration or Recompense, that he might justly wave and not execute the Law of Works, but give Man a new and milder Law of Grace, or Terms of Life; which clearly tends in a great measure to destroy, or make void the Law, instead of making it honorable, by Christ's perfect Conformity to it, in our Nature and Stead; nor can the Righteousness of the Law be said to be fulfilled in us (if what these Men say be true) that is in our nature, or as some read it for us, and indeed if Christ's Obedience and Suffering in our room and stead, hath not delivered us, who believe from the Curse of the Law. Doubtless, we are all under the said Curse still, and so must remain for ever.

Nor can I see why Christ should take our Nature upon him, were he not substituted in our stead, as our Surety to do and suffer.

Besides, how can our Sins be said to be laid upon him, or imputed to him, and his Righteousness imputed to us, were he not put in our stead to do and suffer for us.

If that Righteousness which satisfied the Law of Works, doth not justify us, I know not how we can be justified.

Nor can I see how the Honour of God in his infinite Justice and Holiness, and the Sanction of the Law, is repaired by this Doctrine. But more of this hereafter.

4. These Men do not say that the Righteousness of Christ, whereby he fulfilled the Law, is imputed to us, who believe, to justify us in God's sight; tho' for that Righteousness-sake, God grants us pardon of Sin, and hope of Eternal Life.

But rather (so far as I can gather) that Christ's Righteousness or Obedience is not imputed to us, for which we should be justified and accepted, as being an Obedience due to the Law of the first Covenant; but to his own peculiar Law of a Mediator: But yet so, that Christ's Obedience did merit or purchase; *i.e.* that God should appoint Men new and easier Terms of Life, instead of perfect Obedience, and Death for the failure of that Obedience.

Thus having given you several dangerous, and corrupt Notions of Men about the great Point of Justification, I shall proceed to give you in the last place the true Description, Notion, and Definition of it, according as it hath been, and is asserted generally by all sound Christians and faithful Men.

Eighthly, This is that which we say, *i.e. That Justification is an absolute Act of God's most sovereign Grace, whereby he imputeth the complete and perfect Righteousness of Jesus Christ to a believing Sinner, though ungodly in himself, absolving him from all his Sins, and accepting him as righteous in Christ.*

We affirm that Justification is the Acceptance of a Sinner with God as righteous, through the Righteousness of Jesus Christ imputed to him, not that Justification is nothing more but the pardon of Sin, or the not, or *non*-exacting the Punishment of Sin, due for the breach of the Law of Works, and the acceptance of a Man, so far as he performeth the New Condition of sincere Obedience.

But we affirm that believing Sinners are made partakers of Christ's Righteousness, and the benefits of it; and that by Faith alone, as that by which we wholly fly to him for Righteousness, and trusting in the promise of Life for his Sake and Merits.

'Not that Faith, as one observes, in the whole Latitude, is believing and obeying 'the Gospel, by which we are made Partakers of the benefit of Christ in his 'Obedience to his own Law; and, in that he having purchased this Grant or Law, *i.e.* that they which obey him should be justified and saved, and not that Christ's Obedience shall or doth save them.'

We believe, and teach that by Christ's Righteousness imputed, he that believes is perfectly justified, and is freed from the Curse of the Law, and accepted, and accounted righteous in the sight of God, and hereby hath a certain Title to Eternal Life.

Not that our Justification or Right to Life dependeth wholly upon our Obedience, as the Condition to which it is promised, and we only put into a condition or state of Life imperfect, and subject to change as Obedience itself is: And so that we are not perfectly justified till our Obedience be perfected, which is the Doctrine some Persons of late preach, for as sure as God justifies us, so sure will he save and glorify us, *Rom.* 8.30.

Thus having made our way clear, and removed some Stumbling-blocks, I shall now proceed to show, that all Works done by the Creature are utterly excluded in point of Justification in the sight of God, which must be my business the next day, the time being gone. I shall therefore conclude with a word or two of Application.

1. The First shall be a use of Caution to both Saints and Sinners, to take heed who you hear; it greatly concerns you; for the Times are perilous, the Devil is endeavoring to strike at the Root, even at the Foundation itself, beware lest you are deceived and carried away with those poisonous and abominable Doctrines that are fomented at this present time in and about this City. We ought to keep clean from all Errors; but especially such as are Capital ones. I am afraid many good Christians are not sensible of the sad danger they are in. I cannot see but that the Doctrine some Men strive to promote, is but little better than Popery in a new Dress. Nay one of the worst branches of it too. Shall any who pretend to be true Preachers of the Gospel, go about to mix their own Works or their sincere Obedience with Christ's Righteousness; nay, to put their Obedience in the room and place of

Christ's Obedience, as that in which they trust and desire to be found?

2.   Let me exhort you all to stand fast in that precious Faith you have received; particularly about this great Doctrine of Justification, give your selves to Prayer, and to the due and careful study of God's Word.   And *beware lest ye also being led away with the error of the wicked, fall from your own steadfastness. But grow in Grace, and in the knowledge of our Lord and Saviour Jesus Christ.   To him be Glory both now and for evermore.   Amen.* 2 Pet. 3.17,18.

JUSTIFICATION
without WORKS.

Rom. IV.5. But to him that worketh not,
&c.

I have already opened this Text of Scripture, and gave you an account of the Scope and Coherence thereof at large; and then observed two Points of Doctrine therefrom. First, That all Works done by the Creature are quite excluded, in Point of Justification of a Sinner in the sight of God.

THE last Day, I showed you *divers erroneous Principles* held by some Men about the Doctrine of Justification. I shall trouble you with no Repetition of what we have said, but proceed to what was then propounded to be further done, which is to give you the Scripture-Proofs and Arguments to confirm the Truth of the first Point of Doctrine: viz. *That all Works done by the Creature are quite excluded, &c.*

1. My first Argument shall be taken from the very Letter and express Testimony of the Holy Scripture, *Rom. 3.27. Where is boasting then? It is excluded. By what Law? Of Works? Nay, but by the Law of Faith.* This Text almost in so many Words confirms this Proposition; if all boasting is excluded, all Works are excluded: But more of this hereafter. See *Rom. 4.2 If Abraham were justified by Works, he had whereof to glory, but not before God.* If he had been justified by Works, he had whereof he might glory; but he had nothing to glory in before God.

Therefore he was not justified by Works, *v. 6. Even as David describeth the Blessedness of the Man unto whom God imputeth Righteousness without Works.* He brings in *David* to confirm this great Gospel-Truth. *Psal. 32.1.* And though *David* doth not use the very same Words, as here expressed by the Apostle; yet they are Words of the same Purport, the sense and meaning of *David* is the same.

I wonder at the boldness of some Men, who affirm the Word imputation of Righteousness is no where to be found in the Scripture. Doth not the Apostle plainly and positively assert that God imputeth Righteousness to a Man, and that too without Works. See *Gal. 2.16. Knowing a Man is not justified by the Works of the Law, but by the Faith of Christ.*

Knowing; That is, being sure and certain of this, this is a Doctrine (as if he should say) we are well grounded in, and confident of, That a Man is not justified by the Works of the Law; Works do not justify or declare us righteous in the sight of God: So *Eph. 2.8,9. By Grace ye are saved through Faith, and that not of your selves; 'tis the gift of God, not of Works, lest any Man should boast.* Here it is again in the Affirmative, it is by Grace; and also laid down in the Negative, *not of Works*, and the Reason subjoined.

To these Proofs of Holy Scripture, I might mention That in *Phil. 3.8,9. Yea doubtless, and I account all things but loss for the Excellency of the knowledge of Jesus Christ my Lord, for whom I have suffered the loss of all things, and do count them but dung that I may win Christ, and be found in him, not having my own Righteousness which is of the Law, but that which is through the Faith of Christ, the Righteousness which is of God by Faith.*

What was it *Paul* accounted but Dung, and gave up for Loss? Why, he tells you it was whatsoever he accounted once for gain, or did esteem of, and rested upon; *viz.* all his own Righteousness, while he was a *Pharisee*, and all his other external and legal Privileges, which in times past he gloried in; but now they were nothing to him: He saw no Worth or Excellency in them; but wholly threw himself on Christ, and on his Righteousness for Justification. *I count now as this very time* all the Righteousness I have (he speaks in the present Tense) *but as dung,* that is, in comparison of that Righteousness, which doth and must justify him in God's sight, in which he would be found now, and at Death and Judgment. Compare this Text with that in *Titus 3.5. Not by works of righteousness that we have done; but according to his Mercy he saved us.*

Obj. *But perhaps some will object, that the Apostle in all these places only excludes the works of the Law.*

Answ. 'Tis evident he excludes all Works done by the Creature, either before Grace, or after Grace, as well Works of Obedience to the Gospel as to the Law. Pray observe, *not by works of righteousness that we have done.* We that are Saints, we who profess the Gospel; nay, such Works, *which God hath prepared* or ordained that we should *walk in them.* Eph. 2.9,10. Good Works done by Saints and godly Persons cannot justify them in God's sight. Were not the *Galatians* Christians and Professors of the Gospel, who held without Faith in Christ, no doubt, that they could not be justified? But yet were so far fallen from the true Faith, as to look to be justified also by the Law, or by their Obedience to it; or by an inherent Righteousness, which the Apostle strenuously opposed. Works are indifferently mentioned, as being excluded: *He that is said to be justified by faith, is said not to work, but to have a Righteousness imputed; therefore all works are excluded in this respect.*

2. If all Works were not excluded; then there would still be the same cause or reason to glory, or to boast, be they either *Legal* or *Gospel works;* but since all boasting is excluded, all Works are excluded: It signifies nothing what Works they are, if the reason of their Exclusion be but considered; which is to take away all manner of boasting, and to

abase the Creature, and wholly to magnify God and exalt Free Grace.

3. Moreover the like Debt would be due to us; *For to him that worketh, is the reward not reckoned of grace but of debt.* What though some of my Works doth not make God a Debtor to me? Yet if any Works in this case are not excluded, God would still become a Debtor to me, which is inconsistent with the Doctrine of Free Grace.

4. If Works going before Justification, are excluded from being any cause thereof, then much more those Works that follow Justification, for Causes (as one well observes) do not use to follow after, but go before their Effects, at least in order of Nature.

5. If Works justify, they must of necessity be good Works; but works done before Faith, or without Faith, are not good Works; for *whatsoever is not done of Faith is Sin*, and are dead Works. Neither can the Fruit be good, as our Saviour saith, while the Tree is bad, *Every evil Tree bringeth forth evil fruit*; But every Man before he is justified is like an evil Tree, and therefore can bring forth no good Fruit, no good Works; wherefore all Works, 'tis evident, before Faith and Justification, are utterly excluded.

6. Furthermore, the Apostle speaketh of all Men, whether converted or unconverted, that 'tis not of Works, or Works done by them, or either of them, that they are justified, or saved, *but by grace; we are justified by grace*, and not by Works; all Works are opposed (by the Apostle) to Grace,

therefore all Works are excluded. From hence take this Argument.

That Doctrine that gives the Holy Scripture the Lie, is false and to be rejected.

But the Doctrine that mixes any Works of Righteousness done by the Creature with Faith or the Free Grace of God, in point of Justification, gives the Scripture the Lie; therefore that Doctrine is false, and to be rejected.

2 Arg. That all Works done by the Creature, are utterly excluded in point of Justification appears from the different Nature of Works, and Grace; 'tis positively said, we are justified by Grace.

Now Grace and Works (let Works be of what sort they will) are directly contrary; the one to the other. See *Rom. 11.6. And if it be of Grace, then it is not of Works, otherwise Grace is no more Grace; but if it be of Works, then it is no more of Grace, otherwise work is no more work.* There is no mixing Works and Free Grace together, but one of these doth and will destroy the Nature of the other; and as it holds true in Election, so in Justification: If Justification was partly of Grace, and partly by Works done by the Creature, or from foreseen Holiness and sincere Obedience done by us; then Grace is no more Grace, or Works no more Works: For whatsoever proceeds of Grace (as our Annotators observe) that cometh freely, and is not of Debt. 'But whatsoever cometh by Works, that cometh by Debt; but now Debt and Free Grace, or that which is free and absolutely by Grace, and that which is by Desert, are quite contrary things; therefore to say Men are called and justified, partly by Grace, and partly by Works done by the Creature, this were to put such things together as cannot agree; for 'tis to make Merit no Merit, Debt no Debt, Work no Work, Grace no Grace; and so to affirm and deny one and the same thing. From hence take this Argument:

That which is of the Free Grace of God, is not by any Works done by the Creature. But Justification is of the Free Grace of God; therefore not by any Works done by the Creature. That being justified by his Grace we should be made Heirs according to the hope of Eternal Life, Tit. 3.5. From hence rises all the hopes we have of Salvation; 'tis by, or according to the Free Grace of God, through the Merits of Jesus Christ alone.

3 Arg. My third Argument, to prove all Works done by the Creature are excluded in Justification, is this, viz. *Faith is the way prescribed in the Gospel in order to Justification,* not Love, not Charity, not Works of Mercy, but *Faith.* Now why is Faith rather than any Grace mentioned as the way to be justified; is it not from the Nature of this Grace? In respect of the Object it flies unto, or takes hold of, Faith contrary to any other Grace of the Spirit, carries the Soul out of himself to Christ, like as those who were stung with the fiery Serpents in the Wilderness, were healed by *looking up to the Brazen Serpent.* So by fixing our Eye upon Christ, looking by Faith upon Christ, we come to be healed and justified. Moreover, pray wherein doth the Terms of the Gospel differ from the Terms of the Law, *Do this and live;* or, *The Man that doth these things shall live in them,* Gal. 3.12. Lev. 18.5.

These are the Terms of the Law. Thus runs the *Tenor of the Law.*

But the *Terms* of the Gospel are quite different; *Believe on the Lord Jesus and thou shalt be saved,* Acts 16.31. This was the Doctrine *Paul* preached to the poor trembling *Jailor,* which agrees *with what* the same Apostle says, *Rom.* 10.9. *If thou shalt confess with thy Mouth the Lord Jesus, and shalt believe in thine heart God hath raised him from the dead, thou shalt be saved.* This Confession, and this Faith, has more in it 'tis true than some believe; 'tis not a verbal Confession only, or a bare believing Christ was raised from the dead; *'Tis a believing with all the heart,* Acts 8.37. or to throw our selves wholly on Christ *by the Faith of the Operation of God,* Col. 2.12,13. in full confidence and assurance that he was raised from the Dead as our Head, Surety, and Representative, for our Justification, by the Power or Virtue of which Faith, we also rise with him from a Death in Sin to walk in newness of Life. From hence I argue thus:

That Doctrine which confoundeth the Terms of the Law and Gospel together in point of Justification, is a false and corrupt Doctrine. But the Doctrine that mixeth sincere Obedience, or Works of any kind done by us, with Faith in point of Justification, confound the Terms of the Law and Gospel together in point of Justification; therefore that Doctrine is false and a corrupt Doctrine.

Obj. May be our Opposers will object, that the Terms of the Law consist in perfect Obedience, and that the Terms of the Gospel consist in Faith and sincere Obedience; and therefore they do not confound the Law and gospel together, &c.

Answ. 1. The difference betwixt the Law and the Gospel (as all our true Protestant Divines teach) doth not at all consist in this; *i.e.* that the one requires *perfect Obedience,* and the other *only sincere Obedience,* but in this, that the one requires doing: *Do this and live;* but the other, no doing but believing for Life and Salvation: their Terms differ not only in degree, but in their whole Nature.

3. The Apostle, 'tis evident, opposeth the believing; required in the Gospel to all manner of doing or working for Life, as the Condition proper to the Law, *The Law is not of Faith, but the Man that doth them shall live in them.* Faith in Jesus Christ the Mediator, is not commanded by the Law by which the Soul shall live, the Law saith nothing of this; this is not of the Law: And the Gospel speaks nothing of doing or working for Life, neither of perfect nor sincere Obedience, but the direct contrary, *He that worketh not, but believeth on him that justifieth the Ungodly,* his Faith; not his Obedience to the Gospel, but his Faith is counted for Righteousness.

If therefore we seek Justification by any manner of doing or Works, though upon never so easy and mild a Condition of Obedience, we do thereby bring our selves under the Terms of the Law; which is a complete Declaration of the only Terms whereby God will judge all, and condemn all who are not brought to see the Insufficiency that is in it, *through the Flesh,* Rom. 8.3. to justify the Soul, and from that sight and sense disown all their Works of Obedience, and accept of Christ his Righteousness and perfect Obedience to the Law, to justify them in the sight of God; for let our Obedience be never so sincere, if it be not perfect, we are still Debtors to the Law, and are accursed by it, unless we believe in Jesus Christ; so that all who seek for Justification or Eternal Life knowingly, or ignorantly by any Works done by them less or more, whether commanded by the Law or Gospel, confound the Terms of the Law and Gospel together.

And to this, let me add one thing more, *i.e.* it cannot be rationally doubted, but that the *Jews* and *Judaizing Christians* in the Apostles Days, against whom he contended, did profess any hope to be justified by a complete or perfect Obedience to the Law according to the *rigor of it*; but no doubt thought if they did sincerely do what they could *to love God, and keep his Commandments*, they should be accepted and justified in his sight: For the Jewish Religion taught them that professed it (as one observes) to acknowledge themselves Sinners, which appears by their *Anniversary Humiliation at the day of Atonement*, and several other Rites of the Law; nor have we any reason to conclude but some of them yielded also sincere Obedience (I speak of Moral Sincerity) to the Law; this being so, I see not why their sincere Obedience might not justify them as far forth, as an sincere Obedience to the Gospel or milder Law can a Christian now. Brethren, this new Doctrine is but a piece of *Old Judaism.* These Men do but stumble at the *Old Stumbling-Stone*, which was the seeking to be justified by a man's own Righteousness, in a sincere or upright

Obedience to that Law or Rule of Life God gave them; and so thereby *not submitting themselves to the Righteousness of God,* which is by Faith in Jesus Christ, without the law or any Obedience of ours.

Moreover, pray consider that *Paul* who told the *Galatians they were fallen from Grace,* did not disown Jesus Christ; they were still Professors of the Gospel, though they thought Obedience to the Law a necessary Condition in order to Justification also. Nor was the Observation of the Moral Law a damning Sin: No, no, the Gospel obliges to it; but it was their seeking Justification thereby, and not by Faith only, or in that respect mixing Works with Faith.

4. *All Works done by the Creature are excluded in point of Justification of a Sinner in the sight of God, because we are justified by a perfect Righteousness: If no Man is in himself perfectly righteous, then no Man can be justified by any Works done by him.* But the Apostle proves, that the Justice of God requires a perfect or sinless Righteousness in point of Justification; and also proves that all have sinned, *nor is there one that doeth good, and sinneth not:* No Person has a perfect Righteousness of his own. Alas, Sirs, the Law of God is but as a Transcript, or written Impression of that Holiness, and Purity that is in his own Nature, and serveth to show us what a Righteousness we must be found in, if we are ever justified in his sight. Nor can it be once supposed by any Man, unless blinded, that God will ever loose or relax the Sanction of his Holy Law, or abate a jot or tittle of that Righteousness his Holy Nature and Law

requires in point of our being justified in his sight, it must be all fulfilled by us in our own Persons, or by our Surety for us, and imputed to us.

The Law did not only proceed from God, doubtless, as an Act of his Sovereign Will and Prerogative, but as an Act proceeding from his infinite Justice and Holiness. Can any be so left, as once to conclude God sent his Son to destroy the Law, or to diminish, or take away the least part or tittle of that Obedience he therein enjoins, which so well agrees with the Perfections of his own pure Nature, 'tis strange to me any should conceive God should give way to relax or abrogate the Law of perfect Obedience; nay, send his Son to do it (and in its room bring in a Law for imperfect Obedience to justify us) as if he repented he ever gave it.

For by this means saith a learned Author, God should lose much Honour in making this second Covenant, and granting such easy Terms: for there is no comparison betwixt perfect Obedience required by the Law and due to God as our Creator, and that imperfect Obedience, which is accepted by the Gospel, neither in Quantity, Quality nor Duration: Here it is possible a Man may be converted at the last hour and saved, though he have lived in Rebellion against God many years; What little Honour or Service hath God from such a Man? Yea, from the best Men, who confess *their righteousness to be as filthy rags*, in comparison of a sinless Nature and perfect Life. In respect of all Duties, Time, and Place, without mixture of any sinful Imperfections. What should be the reason of this alteration? *If there had been a Law given, which could have given Life, verily righteousness should have been by the Law,* Gal. 3.21.

Could not Man keep the Law of Works then? It seems the first Law was too strict. This reflecteth upon the Wisdom and Justice of God: It must be granted that perfect Man could observe a perfect Law, had God pleased to give him Grace and Assistance sufficient to his State and Necessity; and so there was no need the Law should be altered, and the Obedience, the Condition of it, changed from perfect to imperfect: For if perfect Man could not keep the Law of perfect Obedience, with sufficient Grace, How should sinful Man perform the Law of sincere Obedience, having no more than sufficient Grace to assist him? Did not God foreknow that Man would break the Law of Works, and so was necessitated to make a New and more easy Law? Or, did not God both foreknow and permit the Fall of Man? Or, could he not have hindered it? Why then should he give way to the abrogating the Command of perfect Obedience, to bring in that of imperfect? Surely (as *Augustine* saith) *God is so Just that he can allow no Evil,* and so Good that he can permit no Evil, except it be with design to bring greater Good out of it. If God permitted the First Covenant to be broken, that thereby he might abase Man and magnify his own Grace, and his Son, in bestowing Heaven freely on him, and in bringing him thither by the continued Power of pardoning and sanctifying Grace; hereby indeed God doth advance his own Glory, by the change of the Covenants.

But that the Condition of perfect Obedience, being broke by Man's Sin; the Law therefore should be disannulled, and a new way of treating with man set up, wherein still Man should be something, and his Works bring about his own Salvation, and God be contented with few and very imperfect Acts of Obedience; this certainly is a prejudice to his Honour; nor doth this make it up, *i.e.* That our Obedience is accepted for Christ's sake, for Christ only made way for removing the Old Covenant, (say you) and the granting a new; but he did not obey in our stead; 'nor doth add any Worth to our Obedience; unless you will say that we are Justified by our own sincere Obedience, the righteousness of Christ making up the defects of it; and so our own righteousness will be a co-ordinate cause of our Justification with the righteousness of Christ; we say,

When the Apostle saith, *By the Works of the Law no Flesh shall be Justified,* he doth not mean only the Law, as in the Hands of *Moses*; but also as it is anew given forth by Jesus Christ; for we are still under Obedience to the *Moral Law,* the substance of which *is to Love God and our Neighbour as our selves.* By the Law is meant that Rule of Life God hath given, whether as written in the heart, or given by *Moses,* or as the Law given by Christ, as well *as it was given by Moses,* no Man, because a Sinner, can be Justified by his own Works, Righteousness, or Obedience; but all Men are

Sinners, whether Professors or Profane, *Rom. 3.23.* (As I said before) he that is justified, *must be just or without Sin,* or have such a Righteousness imputed to him, *God will in no wise clear the guilty,* Exodus 34.7. God is just as well as gracious, *Rom.* 3.26. He cannot suffer any wrong to be done to his Holy Law. Consider the Purity of his Nature and Rectitude of his Will: His Justice must be satisfied, his Law fulfilled by us, or by our Surety for us, and will not abate a tittle of that Righteousness it doth require; yet such is also his Goodness, that what we could not do in keeping perfectly the Law, he sent his Son in our Nature, as our Surety and Representative, to do it for us. *Rom. 8.3. That the Righteousness of the Law might be fulfilled in us,* that is in our Head, who by Faith is ours; and thus by Faith *we do not make void the Law, but establish it.* Is the Law rendered useless, or of none effect by Faith? Are we justified without regard had to the just Commands thereby required, or without a Compensation made for the breach thereof? Is it made void? *No, God forbid,* (saith the Apostle) *we establish the Law,* in as much as by Faith we get or attain to a perfect Righteousness; even such a Righteousness as the Law requires, by being Interested in the complete and perfect Righteousness, and Obedience of Christ to the Moral Law, in whom every Type and Shadow of the Ceremonial Law, and in whom each Promise, and Prophecy is fulfilled also: To close this, take this Argument, *If we are justified by a complete and perfect Righteousness; then an imperfect though a sincere*

Righteousness, doth not justify us, but we are justified by a complete and perfect Righteousness. Ergo,

Remember, Sinners, you are guilty, and must be justified in a way of Righteousness, as well as pardoned in a way of Sovereign mercy, *that God might be just, and the Justifier of them that believe in Jesus,* Rom. 3.26. We can only be justified, saith learned *Leigh, by that Righteousness which is universal and complete. Leigh's* Body of Divinity, *p. 529.* Our Obedience, though sincere, is not universal nor complete; therefore our sincere Obedience or Righteousness justifies us not in God's sight.

5. *All Works done by the Creature are excluded in point of Justification of the Sinner before God, appears because Gospel-Justification is a great Mystery,* and the preaching of it counted Foolishness to the wise Men of this World: to preach Christ and his Righteousness, as that which justifies us they cannot understand; Natural Light and Reason comprehends it not. What, must we be justified by the Obedience and Righteousness of another? This to the learned *Greeks* was a strange Doctrine.

But to say a Man is justified by sincere Obedience, *i.e.* by believing the Truth of God's Word, and living a godly Life, suits well with Man's natural Wisdom and Reason: But the Doctrine of Faith, though it be not against human Reason; yet it is above it, and wholly depends upon divine or super-natural Revelation, *through this Man is preached unto you remission of Sins, and by him all that believe are justified from all things, by which they could not be justified by the Law of Moses,* Acts 13.38,39. *For as by one*

Man's Disobedience many were made Sinners, so by the Obedience of one shall many be made righteous, Rom. 5.19. How dare any say our Works or sincere Obedience is our Righteousness, when the Apostle positively asserts, We are made righteous by the Obedience of Jesus Christ? If it be by his Obedience, 'tis not by our own: For as *Adam's* Sin was imputed to his Seed to *Condemnation;* so is the Obedience or Righteousness of Christ imputed to all those who believe in him to *Justification.*

Now the worst of Men that have any sense of Religion, are prone to conclude the only way to obtain God's Favour, and to be justified in his sight, is to make the practice of Holiness and upright Walking a Condition; nay, the only way thereunto, and that Happiness is to be by that means obtained. Hence 'tis, when they meet with any awakening Convictions or Terror of Conscience, they presently begin to think they must amend their Lives, and perform Religious Duties: Nay, this way the *Heathens* were brought to their best Devotion (as a learned Writer observes) Mankind being made and born under a Covenant of Works, are naturally led to work of Life, or to do something to procure God's Acceptance, and escape his Displeasure. The very Light of natural Reason informs us, that it is just with God to require us to perform Duties of sincere Obedience, or Duties of natural or instituted Religion; and if we fail in doing what our Consciences tell us we ought to do, we presently through self-love and blind hope, persuade our selves God being gracious will pardon us wherein we come short, through Christ, who died for Sinners.

And thus we may perceive that the Persuasion of Salvation and Justification by the Condition of sincere Obedience, hath its Original from our corrupt, natural Reason, and is part of the Wisdom of the World; but *it is none of the Wisdom of God in a Mystery, yea that hidden Wisdom God hath ordained before the World began to our Glory:* It is not of the things of the Spirit of God, nor of the Mystery of Faith, which the natural Man cannot receive, but are Foolishness unto him: This is not *the foolishness of preaching whereby God is pleased to save them that believe,* 1 Cor. 2.6,7,9,14.

Certainly the Justification of a Sinner in the sight of God by Faith only, or to believe on him that justifies the Ungodly, is one of the chief Mysteries of the Gospel; but if our Justification was by our own Obedience, or by conforming our Lives to the Rules of the Gospel, Justification and Salvation would cease from being any more a Mystery: But to be justified by the Righteousness of another, though Sinners in our selves, and have done nothing to procure such Favour and Acceptance at God's hand, can't enter into the heart of natural and self-deceived Mortals. Sirs, our Justification is a great Mystery, as 'tis an Act of God's Sovereign Grace and Wisdom: Herein his Justice and Mercy equally shine forth, and the one doth not eclipse the Glory of the other; Sin is punished, and the Sinner acquitted.

6. Arg. If when we have done all we can do, are unprofitable Servants; then by our best Works of Obedience and Services under the Gospel, we cannot be justified: But contrariwise all Works in that respect, as done by us, are excluded, *Luke* 17.10.

He is no unprofitable Servant, whose Works or sincere Obedience commends him to God in point of Justification: no Man is able to come up full to discharge his Duty: If therefore sincere Obedience instead of perfect, God now requires of us in the case of Justification, and we are able fully to discharge the Law of sincere Obedience, which our new Doctors must say, or they say nothing: then it follows that all such Persons are not unprofitable Servants; for they have done all that God requires of them: Nor indeed can I see (as a Divine observes) if 'sincere Obedience' be the Condition of Justification and Life, how the Imperfections of the Godly should be any Sins against the Gospel, *Where there is no Law, there is no Transgression;* For this New Law, *i.e.* the Gospel, requires no more than sincere and upright Obedience, (say they) though the Law did; and the Gospel also promises Life in like manner to sincere Obedience, as the Law did to perfect and complete Obedience; they may be Imperfections (saith he) in Nature, but not proper Sins. *Prater, non contra Legem,* as the Papists say. If they say, that more than sincere Obedience is required of us, but not as a Condition of Life, I ask by what Law? The Covenant of Works required nothing but as the Condition of Life, no more doth the Gospel, if it be a Law of Life. (After such a manner) our Saviour, doubtless by his Expressions shows us, that all we do avails us nothing in point of Desert, though never so sincerely performed; and therefore far from justifying us in God's sight, but that all we have is of God's Free Grace.

7. *Arg.   Because we are said to be justified by the Righteousness of God: Hence it follows that all our Works of Obedience are excluded*, Rom. 3.21,22. *'Tis called the Righteousness of God in opposition to the Righteousness of the Creature*; not the Essential Righteousness of God, but the Righteousness of Christ the Mediator, who is God as well as Man; and that Righteous God in his infinite Wisdom hath found out to discharge us guilty and condemn'd Sinners, and to justify us in his sight. Hence St. *Paul* renounced all his own Righteousness, that he might be found in the Righteousness of God which is by Faith in Jesus Christ, *Phil.* 3.8,9,10.

Obj.   *But say some* Paul *speaks only of that Righteousness which he had whilst a Pharisee, or of the Righteousness of the Law.   He intends not* (saith Mr. *Williams, p.* 204,205) *Gospel-sincerity, but those Jewish things, or what they boasted of, And again he saith, It was not Gospel-holiness which he counted dung or loss.*

Answ. 1. 'Tis strange this Man should adventure to give such a sense of this Text, when at the same time he would fain have his Reader believe he owns the imputed Righteousness of Christ for our Justification, *p.* 202. 'Tis evident he does deny that the Righteousness of Christ alone is imputed to us for our Justification, as being the only Matter that justifies us from all things, and that without any

Works done by us, either in respect of answering the Rules of the Law or Gospel, though never so sincerely performed. All indeed that I can find he means, is this, *i.e.* That Christ's Merits are the Cause of the Gospel Rule and Promise, and his Righteousness imputed is the Cause for which we are justified and saved, when we have got new Hearts, and answer the Rule of the Gospel in Holiness and sincere Obedience. And thus though imperfect Obedience to the Law was Dogs meat; yet imperfect Obedience to the Rule of the Gospel or Promise thereof, if sincere, is the Children's Bread, nay, that which they ought to seek Justification by, and to desire to be found in. If this Man's Doctrine may be received, it should appear by him that Christ's Righteousness imputed, and our Gospel-obedience mixed together, justifies us: But the chief part is our Conformity to the Rule of sincere Obedience, and Christ's Righteousness, cannot do by Faith alone without this of ours.

2. But Soul know, and be not deceived, this Text hath always been urged by sound Protestant Writers, as one of the Pillars of the Doctrine of Justification by the Righteousness of Christ applied by Faith *alone.* St. *Paul* doth not only disclaim his Righteousness he had before Conversion, or his Obedience to the Law in point of Justification; but he speaks in the present Tense, *What things were gain to me, those have I counted loss for Christ:* But that which he adds, is more, *I do count all things loss.* He speaks, as our Divines note, of all, both past, long since, and also now present, whether Righteousness of his

own, in Obedience to the Law, or Works done by him under the Gospel, all he counted as dung in comparison of the knowledge of Christ and his Righteousness, or the Righteousness of God which is by Faith.

3. 'Tis to be noted how Mr. *Williams* and *Bellarmine* do jump together, and agree in their Exposition of this Text: The latter saith, *That by Righteousness, which is of the Law, are meant Works of Obedience done through the Knowledge of the law by the only strength of natural Abilities before his Conversion.* To which *Chemnitius* and other Protestant Writers answer, That *Paul* rejected not only his Works before His Conversion, which he signifieth, speaking of the time past, *v.*7, but also the Works of his present Condition; *yea, doubtless, and I do count all things but loss.*

Mr. *Williams* saith, *They were the Jewish Privileges, and that conceited Christless Righteousness which he once valued.* But saith he, *a Gospel-holiness is not here intended;* and that still by speaking in the present Tense, *Paul* means what was past, saith he. Pray observe they both exclude the Righteousness of the Law, done by natural or legal Abilities; and they both agree to include an inherent Righteousness, performed by gracious Assistance under the Gospel. This Man is I hope no Papist, though he strives, 'tis plain, to maintain one of the grossest parts of *Popery*, and that part God raised up holy *Luther* principally to detect. Christians look about you, for you are greatly concerned.

4. Consider that the Apostle positively disclaims all Righteousness of Obedience done by the Creature in Justification before God, and did rely on the Righteousness of God: For if he sets our Righteousness, or the Righteousness of the Creature in direct opposition to the Righteousness of God, which is by Faith, then *that which is the Righteousness of God applied by Faith, is not the Righteousness of the Creature, though never so sincerely performed, but the former is true:* Ergo,

5. 'Tis such a Righteousness *Paul* here intended, that he desired to be found in both at Death and Judgment; but durst he, think you, desire to be found in any Righteousness of his own at that Hour, or in that great and dreadful Day? As to this, take what *Reverend Downham,* and others say, 'When a Man shall be 'summoned to appear before the Judgment seat of God, shall seriously consider 'with himself what he shall oppose to the Accusations of Satan, to the Convictions of 'the Law, to the 'Testimony of his own Conscience, confessing himself to be a most 'wretched Sinner, to the Judgment of God, and most righteous Judge, if he look 'back on his own Conversation, as having nothing to trust to but his own 'Righteousness, he shall find 'sufficient Matter of Despair. He may say with *Anselm, Terret me vita mea,* &c. My Life doth terrify me. Alas! what Man is fully able to say he is perfect, or that he sincerely has done all his Duty, in respect of that milder Law of Obedience which they talk of?

Sirs, there is no way in order to Peace of Conscience for us, but to do as *Paul* did, *i.e.* renounce all our inherent Righteousness and Obedience, and fly to the Doctrine of Justification by the Grace of God, through the complete Righteousness of Jesus Christ received by Faith only.

For while a Man (saith he) retains this Opinion, that he can be justified by his own Works, or inherent Righteousness, he can never be soundly persuaded that his Righteousness is sufficient for that purpose; but hath just Cause not only to doubt, but also to despair: And this is the Cause of that *Popish Opinion,* That no Man without *special Revelation* can be assured of the Remission of his Sins in this Life, *Downham on Just. p.* 202. Brethren, some of the Papists themselves have on a Death-bed been forc'd to seek relief, by renouncing all their own Works and Obedience under distress of Conscience and to fly to the Righteousness of Christ, only they kept it close to themselves, lest that *gap being opened, their Trade should fall to the ground,* as appears by the Answer of *Stephen Gardyner* to the *Bishop of Chichester, Foxe's Acts and Mon.* Vol. 2. p. 46. Take two or three Arguments further here, *viz.*

1. If that Righteousness which is the Righteousness of God, which is by Faith, in opposition to the Righteousness of the Creature doth justify us; then all Works done by the Creature are excluded in point of Justification in God's sight: But the former is true; Ergo, *all Works done by the Creature are excluded, &c.*

2. If Paul, nor no other Child of God durst, or dare to be found in any Righteousness of their own at Death or Judgment; then Works done by us, or sincere Obedience justify us not; but the former is true; therefore no Works of ours, nor sincere Obedience doth justify us in God's sight.

3 Arg.   That Doctrine that holds a Christian down under slavish Fear, by grounding his Justification on his own Works of Holiness and sincere Obedience, is not of God; but the Doctrine of Justification by our own Work of Holiness or sincere Obedience, holds a Christian down under slavish Fear, by grounding his Justification on his Works of Holiness and sincere Obedience; therefore that Doctrine is not of God.   Christians take heed what Books you read, if you would have a sound and steadfast ground of Hope, Peace and Comfort, nay, not only have the Joy of God's Salvation, but Salvation itself: For if you build on your own Righteousness or Obedience, and not on the Righteousness of God, which is received by Faith only, you will fall into Hell, *by stumbling at the same stumbling-stone* the *Jews* did, *Rom.* 9.32. *Chap.* 10.2.

8 Arg.   All Works done by the Creature are excluded in point of Justification of a Sinner in the sight of God, because we are justified by that Righteousness by which the Justice of God is satisfied, and his Wrath appeased.   That Righteousness that delivers us alone from Condemnation, and the Curse of the Law, doth justify us and none else; and is not that the Righteousness of Christ? Is not he that is acquitted from Condemnation and Death, put into a state of Justification and Life?

What is it that these new Doctors talk of? How is Christ's Righteousness made our *legal Righteousness*, and yet not our *Evangelical Righteousness*? If the Righteousness of Christ be imputed to us, as that which when apply'd by Faith, delivers us from Condemnation, Wrath and Death, certainly we need no other Righteousness to justify us in God's sight unto eternal Life.

Obj. *But Unbelief is against the Gospel, what Defense against this?*

Answ. The Person that we speak of, hath *Faith*, he *believes in Christ*, therefore the Gospel charges him not, and the Law cannot: *Here is a Pardon, if you receive it, you are acquitted: Here is a Plaster, if you apply it, you are healed.* The Man receives the Pardon, applies the Plaster, he is by the Grace of God helped to believe, he is therefore delivered from Death, and put into a State of Justification, *and shall not come into Condemnation*, Rom. 8.1.

2. No Man is acquitted from the Charge of any Sin, either against the Law or Gospel, till he believes; but when he believes, when he applies the *Merits and Righteousness of Christ*, he is *justified from all Things, from all Sins* of what Nature soever they are. Must we by our sincere Obedience make God a Compensation for the Sins we have committed against the Gospel, and free Tenders of his Grace, or for slighting the Word of Reconciliation? &c. Hath not Christ satisfied God's Justice for all our Sins; and when we believe, are we not thereby justified from all Sins committed against the Gospel, as well as against the Law? Have we any

Plea at God's Bar, but that of the Merits of Christ, and his Righteousness only, let our Sin or Guilt be what it will?

Quest. *But how doth it appear a Man doth believe in Christ indeed.*

Answ. Why his Faith, if true, will *make him a new Creature*, 'twill *purify his heart*, it will lead him into *sincere* and *universal Obedience*; but 'tis Christ's Righteousness still nevertheless that justifies him in God's sight, though his Obedience and inherent Righteousness may justify his Faith, or evidence the Truth of Grace to his own Conscience and to Men also, But,

Obj. *God doth require an Evangelical Righteousness in all that do believe this Righteousness Christ is not, nor is it the Righteousness of Christ; he may be said to be our legal Righteousness, but our Evangelical Righteousness he is not. And so far as we are righteous with any Righteousness, so far we are justified by it; for according unto this Evangelical Righteousness we must be tried, if we have it we shall be acquitted, and if we have it not we shall be condemned; there is therefore a Justification according to it.*

To this, take reverend Dr. *Owen's* Answer, According to some Authors, or maintainers of this Opinion, I see not, saith he, but that the Lord Christ is as much our Evangelical Righteousness as he is our Legal; for our Legal Righteousness, he is not in their Judgment by a proper imputation of his Righteousness unto us, but by the Communication of the Fruits of what he did and suffered for us: And so he is our Evangelical Righteousness also;

for our Sanctification is an Effect or Fruit of what he did and suffered for us, *Eph.* 5.25,26. *Titus* 2.10.

2.   None have this Evangelical Righteousness, but those who are in order of Nature at least justified before they actually have it; for it is that which is required of all that do believe, and are justified; and we need not much enquire how a Man is justified after he is justified.

3.   God hath not appointed this Personal Righteousness, in order to our Justification before him in this Life, though he have appointed it to evidence our Justification before others, &c.

4.   If we are in any sense justified hereby in the sight of God, we have whereof to boast before him: Though we may not *absolutely* in respect of *Merit;* yet we may so *comparatively*, and in respect of others, who cannot make the same Plea for their Justification: *but all boasting is excluded*. And it will not relieve, to say, that this Personal Righteousness is of the Free Grace and Gift of God unto some, and not unto others; for we must plead it as our Duty, and not as God's Grace.   See his further Answer, Dr. *Owen of Justification p.* 221,222.   To close this, take this Argument:

If by that Righteousness of Christ which is out of us, though imputed to us, the Justice of God is fully satisfied, we are justified; then all Works done by us, or inherent in us, are excluded in our Justification before God: But by that Righteousness of Christ which is out of us, though imputed to us, the Justice of God is satisfied; therefore all Works done by us, or inherent in us, are excluded in our Justification before God.

Finally, saith *Bellarmine*, Nothing more frequently doth the Scripture testify than that the Passion and Death of Christ was a full and perfect Satisfaction for Sins. Further he saith, God doth indeed not accept, as a true Satisfaction for Sin, any Justice but that which is infinite, because sin is an infinite Offence, &c. *De Just.* 1.2. Now the Sufferings of Christ and his Righteousness only, is of an infinite Value, ours is not: therefore Christ's Righteousness only, and not ours, is a true Satisfaction for Sin. Our Adversaries sometimes are forc'd to speak the Truth.

9 Arg. All Works done by the Creature, are excluded, &c. Because 'tis by the Obedience of one Man that many are made righteous, that is Jesus Christ, he is made of God unto us righteousness, &c. Rom. 5.18,19. 1 Cor. 1.30. But our inherent Righteousness is of many; *i.e.* every Man's own sincere Obedience that obtains it.

10 Arg. All Works done by the Creature, are excluded in point of Justification I prove thus; If any one Man was justified without Works or sincere Obedience, or through Faith only, then all Works of Obedience, &c. are excluded. But the *Thief on the Cross* was justified without Works of Obedience, and so are all *Infants* that die in Infancy that are saved; the Matter of Justification is one and the same; the *Balsam* that cures our *Malady* is all one in *Infants* and in *Adult Persons*; 'tis Christ's Death, Christ's blood, the Merits of Jesus Christ; or 'tis his active and passive Obedience, which is our only Righteousness to discharge us from Sin and Condemnation: Though the *Mode* or *Manner* of the Application thereof may be different to the *Adult*, 'tis by Faith only; to *Infants* in a more secret and hidden Manner, not known to us.

Nay, *Abraham, David* and *Paul*, were not justified by inherent Righteousness, but by Faith without Works of Obedience, and as *Abraham* was justified, so are all his *spiritual and true Seed*, to them, and every one of them, is Faith imputed to Justification or Righteousness, even by Faith alone without Works as Paul proveth, *Rom.* 4.3-5.

11 Arg. Is, because Christ is tendered or offered to Sinners as Sinners, not as righteous persons, but as ungodly ones, without any previous Qualifications required of them to set themselves to receive Christ; they are all as poor, lost, undone, weary, and heavy laden Sinners required to believe in Christ, or venture their Souls upon him, though they have no Money, no Righteousness; if they have, they must cast it away, in point of Dependence, Trust, or Justification: These are they, Christ came to call; these are they he invites to come to him, these are they *he came to seek and to save*, who see nothing of Good in themselves; but contrariwise, are sensible of their filthy Hearts and abominable Lives: And yet though it be thus, if they come to Christ, they shall at that very instant be justified, which Faith or Divine Grace will soon make them holy and sanctify them; for holy Habits are at that very instant infused into them, though Sanctification is a gradual Work: *This being so, it follows all Works done by the Creature are excluded, in point of Justification of a Sinner before God.* What said *Paul* to the *ungodly Jailor*, when he cry'd out, *Sirs, what must I do to be saved?*

Believe on the Lord Jesus, and thou shalt be saved and thy house, Acts 16.31. The Apostle did not put him upon doing to be saved, but upon believing. But O how contrary is this to the Doctrine some Men preach *now a-days*, they tell Sinners what they must do, *what good Fruits they must bring forth, and this before the Tree is good*, or they have closed with Christ, or have real Union with him; nay, bid the People take heed they do not too soon believe on Christ or venture on Christ. *Sirs*, you cannot too soon believe in Christ, I mean truly believe; I don't say you should get a presumptuous Faith, but true Faith: But is it not strange a Minister should be heard lately to say, *A Man must get a new heart before he can be justified.* I thought a Man could not have *a new Heart* before he had true Faith: Is not a new Heart one of the *absolute Promises of the New Covenant, Ezek.* 36.26. Can any thing, short of *Almighty Power*, make the *Heart new*, or *form the Image of God in the Soul*, or can a Man that hath a new Heart be under Condemnation, for are not all in that Condition who are not actually justified? Or can a dead Man quicken himself, or dead Works please God? Or the Fruit be good before the Tree is good? Are not all that are new Creatures in Christ Jesus, and have union with him, *2 Cor.* 5.17?

12 Arg. With which I shall conclude the Proof of the Doctrine (though I might mention many more, to prove *all Works done by the Creature, or Obedience of his, are in this Case excluded, &c*) It is, *because if a Man should so walk as to know nothing of himself*, i.e. *be so righteous, or so sincere in his obedience, as not to have his Conscience to accuse, or reproach him; yet he cannot thereby be justified.* See what *Paul* saith, *Though I know nothing of my self, yet am I not thereby justified,* 1 Cor. 4.4. Though he had kept a Conscience void of Offence towards God, and towards Men; yet in the Point of Justification, he renounces all his own Obedience and Righteousness that was inherent in him. Durst holy *Job* depend upon his Sincerity, or venture in that, to stand at God's Tribunal? Though he could plead Uprightness against the false Charge of his three Friends, and with much Confidence persevere therein, justifying his Sincerity with his Faith and Hope in God; against their Accusations, he *showed his Faith by his Works,* and stands on his Justification of himself against Hypocrisy. But at length he is called into the immediate Presence of God, to plead his own Cause; not now as it was stated between himself and his Friends before, Whether he were sincere or not. The Question was now reduced to this, *i.e.* on what grounds he might, or could be justified *in the sight of God*; and God to prepare him in this Case, and to show him what to plead at his bar, graciously manifested himself unto him. And quickly now he comes to see all his former Pleas, as Dr. *Owen* notes, of *Faith, Hope, and sincere Obedience,* would not avail him; but he is made to fly under the deepest Self-abasement and Abhorrency to Sovereign Grace and Mercy; *For then Job answered the Lord, and said, I am vile, what shall I answer thee? I will lay mine hand upon my mouth: Once have I spoken, but I will not answer; yea twice, but I will proceed no further,* Job 40.3,4,5. *I have heard of thee by the hearing of the Ear; but now mine Eye seeth thee: Wherefore I abhor my self, and repent in Dust and Ashes.* Dr. Owen.

How, *Job*, abhor thy self! that art so holy, so sincere, such an upright Man? What is all the Beauty of thy inherent Holiness, and sincere Obedience become nothing to thee? *Is it as Dung* now? Darest thou not appear before God in it, nor stand at his Bar thereby to be justified? No, no, he saw that there was Sin cleaving to his best Duties, and that he was vile in God's sight.

Sure this agrees not with Mr. *Daniel William's New Doctrine: It was not Gospel-holiness which Paul counted Dung,* says he. No doubt *Job's Righteousness* was the Fruits of Faith as well as *Paul's,* and purified his Heart too; who says, *He knew that his Redeemer lived,* Job 19:25. But yet for all this Holiness, Uprightness, and sincere Obedience, he *abhors himself, and repents* he ever had such a Conceit of the Worth of his own Righteousness.

Let a Man place himself in the Condition wherein *Job* was to stand before the Bar of God's Justice; and let him attend to the Charge he hath against him, and let him consider what will be his best Plea at God's Tribunal, that he may be justified. I do not believe, (saith the *reverend Doctor,*) that any Many living, hath more encouraging grounds to plead for an Interest in his own Faith and Obedience *in his Justification before God* than *Job* had: Alas, we must all say with *David, Enter not into Judgment with thy Servant; for in thy sight shall no Man living be justified.* This must be our Plea when we come to die, *i.e.* My Trust is in Christ, in his Blood, in his Death, in his Righteousness: This is only pleadable now, and in the Judgment-Day, this will give ease to a convinced, terrified Conscience, that knows the Nature, Holiness, Purity, and Justice of God: We must say with *Anselm, My Conscience hath deserved Damnation, and my Repentance is not sufficient for Satisfaction; but certain it is that thy Mercy aboundeth above all Offences.* The Prophet *Isaiah* cries out, *He was undone,* not withstanding his sincere Obedience, because a *Man of unclean lips, Isa.* 6. When the Day of Judgment or Death comes, all Hands will be weak, and all Hearts faint: Confidence in our own Uprightness will then fail us, because no Works can then be found to answer the Righteousness of God; *If thou shouldst mark Iniquity, who shall stand? O Lord, Righteousness belongs unto thee, but unto us Confusion of face; though I know nothing of my self, yet am I not thereby justified.* No, no, he was justified by the Righteousness of God, by Christ's sinless Obedience, and not by his own imperfect though sincere Obedience; therefore all Works done by the Creature are excluded: 'Tis evident the Godly at the Judgment-Day will not plead their own Righteousness; but contrariwise will then renounce it in this respect, as appears by that, in *Matt.* 25.37. *Lord, when saw we thee an hungered, and fed thee; thirsty, and gave thee drink &c.* They will rather blush and be ashamed to hear any mention of their Works, or of their Obedience, than to plead it at that Day: All the good Works which they have done, will be swallowed up in the Admiration of God's Free and Infinite Grace: But so much as to the Proof of the Doctrine. I shall close with a brief Word of Application.

Application

This reproves all such as go about to eclipse the Doctrine of Free Grace, or of Justification of Faith only, and plead for sincere Obedience, and mix Grace and Works together: Also it may serve to convince all Men, That such Teachers, however cry'd up, are not true Gospel-Ministers; and therefore should be avoided, though they should speak with a tongue like Angels.

1. *Caution.* Do not think, O Soul, that thy own Righteousness doth justify thee, through Christ's Merits; or that Christ's Righteousness is thy *Legal Righteousness*, and not thy *Evangelical.* No, no, he is thy whole Saviour; 'tis Christ's own Arm that brought Salvation, 'tis not our own Righteousness joined or coupled with the Merits and Righteousness of Christ; but his Personal Righteousness only received by Faith. And,

2. Take heed you do not put Faith itself in the room (as your Act, or as a Divine Habit, or as the Product thereof) of perfect Obedience; for 'tis Christ's Righteousness that is put in the place or room of that perfect Obedience which God required of us in Point of Justification: Faith only

justifies, in respect of the Object it apprehends and takes hold of.

3.   Tremble ye who trust in your Moral, or Gospel-Obedience, your Acts of mercy, or good Deeds, and holy Lives.   Tremble ye who rest on your Duties, who glory in your knowledge, and outward Privileges; you fast, and pray, and hear Sermons, and so you may, and go to Hell at last; notwithstanding, these things you must do, but yet not seek to be justified thereby; do them as Duties in point of Performance; but lay them down in point of Dependence.

4.   Here is Comfort for Sinners; but if you are self-righteous Persons, or go about like the *Jews* of old, to establish your own Righteousness, down to Hell you will fall, *Rom.* 10.2.   This Doctrine will support you that are weak, and doubt for want of inherent Righteousness, take hold of it, *A Robe of Righteousness*, Put it on, *Believe on Christ*, as poor Sinners come to him, you that have *no Money, no Worth, no Merit, no Righteousness*, this Wine and Milk of Justification and Pardon is for you: Cry to God to help you to believe; Christ is the *Author of your Faith*, 'tis the Gift of God, 'tis a Grace of the Spirit; Do you see you are wounded?   Look to Christ, *Believe, and thou shalt be saved*, Mark 16.16.   John 3.15,16.   If thou can'st not come to God as a Saint, come as a Sinner; nay, as a Sinner thou must come, and may'st come.

Obj.   But this Doctrine is decried for *Antinomianism.*

Answ. They know not what *Antinomianism* is, that thus brand us, as here-after I shall God-assisting prove. If this is to be an *Antinomian*, we must be all such, and let them mock on; the Lord open their Eyes: We are for the Law as *Paul* was, and for Holiness and sincere Obedience, as any Men in the World; but we would have Men act from right Principles, and to a right end: We would have Men act in Holiness, from a Principle of Faith, from a Principle of Spiritual Life, be first *married to Christ that they may bring forth Fruit to God,* Rom. 7.4.

We preach to you, Sinners, that Jesus Christ will entertain you, if you come to him, bid you welcome, and not cast you off, because of the Greatness of your Sins, though you have no Qualifications to recommend you to him. Would you wash your selves from your Sins, and then come to the Fountain of his Blood to be washed; we hold forth Christ to be your whole Saviour, and that he is *set forth as the Propitiation through Faith in his Blood;* whom if you close with, and believe in, you shall be justified. We tell you God justifies the Ungodly, *i.e.* that they are so before justified.

Nor is our Doctrine any other, than what all sound Protestants have always contended for; nay, which the Church of *England* in her 39 Articles doth assert, viz. *Imputed Righteousness and Justification only for the Merits of our Lord and Saviour Jesus Christ by Faith, and not for our own Works and Deservings, and that we are justified by Faith only; and that Works done before the Grace of Christ, and the Inspiration of the Spirit, are not pleasing to God, forasmuch as they spring not from Faith in Christ, neither do they make Men meet to receive Grace, &c.*

Let me exhort you not to receive for Truth all things that you find asserted in some Men's Books, Sermons, and Writings, though recommended by such Men you have so great a Veneration for. I hope some of those Ministers that have set their Hands to *Mr.* Williams *late Book,* will see Cause to repent of their rash Act, and great Inadvertency; for we cannot see but that the said Book brings in another Gospel, or is a Subversion of the Gospel (tho' the unwary Reader may not soon discover the Poison that lies hid in it) and 'tis full of *hard,* and *uncouth,* or *unintelligible Terms, Notions* and *Expressions,* not formerly known to the Christian World: 'Tis strange to me that he should intimate and hold forth the Gospel to be a Law, or Command of Duty, as a Condition with the Sanction of *Threats* upon Non performance, and *Promises of Rewards* upon Performance of *sincere Obedience;* for if Sincerity of Grace and Holiness be not the Condition of that which he often calls the Rule of the Promise, which he nevertheless says is not the Precept, I understand him not: Doth he not mean a Man must be holy, sincere, or a New Creature, before he ventures on the Promise of the Gospel, or can be justified, which is the Error my Text opposes; as if the free Promise of the Grace of God in laying hold on Christ and his Righteousness justifies us not, but that we must get some inherent Qualifications of Holiness, as the Rule of the Promise, before we venture upon it, or throw our selves upon Jesus Christ, and so must receive him *as Saints* and not *as Sinners*, which is directly contrary to what all our true Protestant Writers and *Modern Divines* have all along asserted. *The Papists* say, a Man must be inherently righteous before he can be declared just; and that Faith justifies, as it infuses such a Righteousness in us: And this Man says but little else, if I understand him; *i.e.* a Man must answer the Rule of the Gospel-Promise, asserting that the Gospel doth judicially determine a Conformity to the Rule thereof; and when God forgives, he *judicially* declares a Man hath true Faith, and by Faith he means doubtless more than laying hold on Christ, *viz.* the making good *the Baptismal Covenant, i.e.* to *love, serve, and sincerely to yield Obedience to the Gospel;* so that Faith must by him be taken in a large and comprehensive manner: And that before God declares us righteous to Justification, he looks whether or not we have fully answered the Conditions (according to the Doctrine these Men preach) and finding the Creature has done that, God judicially gives the Promise in a way of Reward; and the Obedience being sincere, though imperfect, 'tis accepted as far forth as perfect Obedience would have been (could it have been performed) under the Law of Works; so that still inherent Righteousness is the Condition of our Justification before the holy God, and not the Righteousness of Christ: Away with this Error.

Brethren, This New Law it seems can give Life upon Obedience thereto, the first being taken away; but *if by the Law, any Law, a Man might be justified,*

Christ is dead in vain: For as one Law, so all Laws of Works since Man hath sinned, utterly fail, and are unable to justify us in God's sight. For as some learned Men have observed, the Greek Word is not *the* Law but *a* Law. Let it be what Law or Rule of Righteousness it will, that requires perfect or imperfect Obedience, it will not do, *Gal.* 3.11. *For the just shall live by Faith:* Justification and Life comes only that way, and not by Works of Obedience we have done.

And truly to talk of sincere Obedience, when performed by an unregenerate Person, 'tis strange Doctrine. Sincerity must only be look'd for in him, who is renewed by the Grace of God: 'Tis as impossible for an unregenerate Person to perform sincere Obedience (if we speak of Gospel-Sincerity) as it is for a Believer to perform perfect Obedience to the Law of Works.

Therefore Sinners, though 'tis your Duty to reform your Lives, and leave your abominable Sins, which often bring heavy Judgments upon you in this World, and expose you to eternal Wrath in the World to come; yet know that all that you can do, will fail in point of your Acceptance and Justification in God's sight, or to save your Souls: Your present Work and Business is to believe in Jesus Christ, to look to him, who only can renew his sacred Image in your Souls, and make you New Creatures, which must be done, or you perish. O cry that he would help your Unbelief: Come, venture your Souls on Christ's Righteousness; Christ is able to save you, though you are never so great Sinners. Come to him, throw your selves at the Feet of Jesus: *Look to Jesus,* who came to seek and save them that were lost; *If any man thirst, let him come to me and drink,* John 7.37,38. You may have Water of Life freely. Do not say I want Qualifications or a Meetness [fitness] to come to Christ. Sinner, dost thou thirst? Dost thou see a want of Righteousness? 'Tis not a Righteousness; but 'tis a sense of the want of Righteousness, which is rather the Qualification, thou shouldst look at: Christ hath righteousness sufficient to clothe you; Bread of Life to feed you, Grace to adorn you; or whatsoever you want, it is to be had in him. We tell you there is help in him, Salvation in him, *through the Propitiation in his Blood* you must be justified, which is by Faith alone.

Know that *God justifies the Ungodly,* not by making them first inherently righteous, nor are they ungodly any more after justified: *The Faith of the Operation of God will soon purify your Hearts,* and cleanse your Lives; this Grace will teach you *to deny all Ungodliness and Worldly Lusts, and to live soberly, righteously, and godly in this present evil World.* We do not tell you, you must be holy, and then believe in Jesus Christ; but that you must believe in him, that you may be holy. You must first have Union with him, before you can bring forth Fruit to God; you must act from Life, and not for Life.

Obj. *But O 'tis hard thus to believe; to be ungodly, and yet to believe; to see no Holiness of our own, no divine Habits planted in us; Had we some degree of Sanctification, or righteousness of our own, we could then believe.*

Answ. Is not Christ able to save you, or is he not willing to save you, unless you are Co-workers and Co-partners with him in your Salvation? Or are you unwilling to be saved, unless you might share with him in the Glory of your Salvation? Is it hard for you to believe the highest Testimony and Witness that ever was born to any truth? Can't you believe the Report of the Gospel, or receive the Record God hath given of his Son? Is resting on Christ hard? Can't you beg for Bread rather than perish? Can't you drink when thirsty, when you are bid to do it freely?

We say the Gospel is not a conditional Covenant of Obedience; or that Faith, and Holiness, or Faith, and Good Works, are the Condition of it, denying we are justified by any Works of ours, as a subordinate Righteousness to the Righteousness of Christ, or that we are justified for Christ's sake only; but not that his righteousness is imputed to us also, as our Sins were imputed or laid upon him. We say that Faith doth not justify as an Act, nor as a Habit, or from any Worth there is in that, *it being only as a hand to apply the Remedy,* we say, Faith is a Fruit of Christ's Purchase; and that *he who spared not his own Son, but delivered him up for us all, will much more give us all things,* that is, Grace here, and Glory hereafter: He that gave us the greatest Gift, will not deny to his Elect ones the lesser Gift.

And now know all you *Pharisaical* Persons, this Doctrine will pull down your high Thoughts and Imaginations, and abase your Pride.

To you that are Believers, Oh! admire Free Grace; lift Christ up who died for you, *the Just for the Unjust,* who bore your Sins, *who was made sin for us that knew no Sin, that we might be made the Righteousness of God in him.* He gave himself for you, and has given Grace, the Fruit of his Death, and himself to you. O labour to be a holy People; live to him that died for you, and rose again.

To conclude. Is there any Sinner here? Are you *ungodly,* and in a wretched Condition (in your own Eyes)? Are you *weary and heavy Laden?* Come to Christ, lift up your Heads: *For to him that worketh not, but believeth on him that justifies the Ungodly, his Faith is counted for Righteousness.*

POSTSCRIPT.

Reader, I have now given thee the Substance of the two first Sermons preached on this Text; and that which follows, contains an Answer to all the main Objections brought against this Doctrine; particularly that of the Apostle *James*, about *Works justifying, and not Faith only*. And if this meets with kind Reception, and I have Encouragement, I shall publish two Sermons more* (God willing) and fully demonstrate, That Justification is by the Imputation of Christ's Righteousness, or by Grace alone; and the Nature of Imputation opened, together how we are to understand the change of Persons: Wherein I shall produce the Testimony of the *ancient Fathers*, and a multitude of our faithful *Modern Divines*, and *worthy late Writers;* that so you may see we plead for no New Doctrine, but the very same that all Good Men and Orthodox Christians, in every Age have maintained, which will, I hope, be of great Advantage to the Church of God. And also show you how Faith is concerned in our Justification, or is said to justify, and how not; together with the Nature of that Faith. As also the Difficulty and Excellency of that Faith that is accounted for Righteousness: Likewise the horrid Evil and Danger of the Sin of Unbelief; and Mr. *Williams's* Book and Doctrine further considered.

*Publisher's Note: *We are hoping to publish the two sermons mentioned by Keach in this Postscript.*

OTHER SGCB TITLES

We are delighted to offer several outstanding books from the past and present that open and apply the Holy Scriptures:

Opening Scripture: *Hermeneutical Manual* by Patrick Fairbairn
The Scripture Guide: *Introduction to Bible Study* by J.W. Alexander
The Poor Man's Old Testament Commentary by Robert Hawker
First Things: *Lessons Upon the First Lessons God Taught Man* by G. Spring
Heroes of Israel: *Abraham, Isaac, Jacob, Joseph & Moses* by W.G. Blaikie
Expository Lectures on the Book of Joshua by W.G. Blaikie
Expository Lectures on the Book of 1st Samuel by W.G. Blaikie
Expository Lectures on the Book of 2nd Samuel by W.G. Blaikie
Lectures upon the Book of Esther by Thomas M'Crie
Pathway into the Psalter by William Binnie
The Poor Man's New Testament Commentary by Robert Hawker
Sabbath Scripture Readings on the NT by Thomas Chalmers
Come Ye Apart: *Devotional Thoughts from the Gospels* by J.R. Miller
Lectures on the Book of Acts by John Dick
Paul the Preacher: *Studies on Discourses in Acts* by John Eadie
Notes on Galatians by J. Gresham Machen
Opening Up Ephesians by Peter Jeffery
A Commentary on the Greek Text of Galatians by John Eadie
A Commentary on the Greek Text of Ephesians by John Eadie
A Commentary on the Greek Text of Philippians by John Eadie
A Commentary on the Greek Text of Colossians by John Eadie
A Commentary on the Greek Text of Thessalonians by John Eadie
Short Explanation of the Epistle to the Hebrews by David Dickson
Exegetical & Expository Commentary on Hebrews by Wm Gouge
A Commentary upon the Epistle of Jude by William Jenkyn

Call us Toll Free at 1-877-666-9469
Send us an e-mail at sgcb@charter.net
Visit us on line at solid-ground-books.com

NEW "BURNING ISSUES" SERIES

SGCB is introducing a new series of titles addressing the *Burning Issues* of our day from the hearts of those on fire for the Lord.

YEARNING TO BREATHE FREE? *Thoughts on Immigration, Islam & Freedom* by David Dykstra

"I have read this book with great interest. His description of the real nature of jihad and its continuing power today is valuable. What he has written is especially important since so many on the upper levels of government continue to claim that Islam is fundamentally a peaceful religion; it is not. Dykstra has made that very clear. I do hope that this book is well accepted. Its main message is sorely needed." - Dr. Joel Nederhood, Now available!

PULPIT CRIMES: *The Criminal Mishandling of God's Word* by James White

James White of Alpha-Omega Ministries is writing what may be his most provocative book yet. White sets out to examine numerous "crimes" being committed in pulpits throughout the land every week, as he seeks to leave no stone unturned. Based firmly upon the bedrock of Holy Scripture, one "crime" after another is laid bare for all to see.." - Now Available!

COMMON FAITH, COMMON CULTURE by Joe Bianchi

"Joseph M. Bianchi has provided an inspiring aerial overview of Christianity's formative salt and light impact on world history. 'it is a culture that transforms societies by transforming people one by one.' Bianchi provides a tonic for believers disheartened by the contemporary darkness of encroaching postmodernism. Surely the gates of Hell will not prevail, for in Christ, we will triumph as more than conquerors. Well done!" -Rev. Mark Chanski, author of *Manly Dominion.* - Now Available!

TWO MEN FROM MALTA by Joel Nederhood & Joe Serge

One of the men is the Apostle Paul, the other is Joe Serge, a Toronto newspaperman. In this book Serge describes his odyssey from Roman Catholicism to the faith of the Reformation. Serge invited Joel Nederhood, a theologian and long time radio and television teacher, to join him in examining primary Roman teaching such as "the Mass," "Mary," "the Papacy," and the essence of salvation itself. This is a warm invitation to Roman Catholics to examine their faith. Due Spring 2007.

Call us Toll Free at 1-877-666-9469
Visit our web site at http://solid-ground-books.com

LaVergne, TN USA
30 October 2009
162541LV00001B/16/A